The Process of Excelling

*The Practical How-To
Guide for Managers
and Supervisors*

Roger Herman

Oakhill Press

Greensboro, North Carolina

This publication is designed to provide accurate and authoritative information in regard to the subject matter covered. It is sold with the understanding that the publisher is not engaged in rendering legal, accounting, or other professional service. If legal advice or other expert assistance is required, the services of a competent professional person should be sought. *From a Declaration of Principles jointly adopted by a committee of the American bar Association and a committee of Publishers.*

10 9 8 7 6 5 4 3 2 1

Library of Congress Cataloging in Publication Data

Herman, Roger E.
The process of excelling
1. Management 2. Excellence 3. Executive Ability. I. Title
HD38.H462 1988   658.4'09   87-63315
ISBN 1-886939-04-7 Paperback
ISBN 1-886939-22-5 Hardcover

Oakhill Press
Post Office Box 787
Summerfield, NC 27358
Printed in the United States of America

Other Books
by Roger E. Herman

Turbulence! Challenges & Opportunities in the
World of Work (1995)

Keeping Good People: Strategies for Solving the
Dilemma of the Decade (1991) (latest edition:
1997)

Emergency Operations Plan (1983)

Disaster Planning for Local Government (1981)

Forthcoming:

Signs of the Times

Lean & Meaningful
                    . . . and more!

Would you like to be notified when Roger Herman's forthcoming books are published? Send a message to his office
(see "About the Author" on page 215) and add your name to
his mailing list.

Dedication

With all the traveling I do, serving clients, learning and relaxing, I have the opportunity to come in contact with hundreds of managers, supervisors, and line employees in the travel and tourism industry. These dedicated professionals at reservation desks, airports, and hotels are representative of todays employment world. Whether they work in the cramped space of an airplane at 35,000 feet or in a bustling restaurant environment, their work makes a big difference to those of us who spend a lot of time away from home "doing our thing."

Contact with their customer is brief, but can be deeply meaningful. Some of these folks are absolutely wonderful; some fall short of our expectations. That's the same as we find in any industry, but customers in the hospitality environment are often under stress, confused, and rather demanding. To all those amazing people who have made my travels more smooth, under often challenging circumstances, thanks!

On behalf of all the consultants and speakers who travel to serve our clients, thank you travel professionals for making it possible for us to make a difference in our world. Even with all the technology in our sped-up world, your personal touch is sincerely appreciated.

To all my colleagues who travel "for whatever reason," next time you have the opportunity, extend a heartfelt "thanks" to these people who put up with so much to smooth our way. And to their managers and supervisors whose behavior has unwittingly inspired some of the comments in this book, please read and apply *The Process of Excelling* to smooth the way for your special people.

Contents

Introduction

The concept of Excellence has almost lost its meaning because it has been overused, misused, and abused. Everywhere you look, something is being described as "excellent," even though in reality it may be far from excellent in the purest sense of the word.

We have been bombarded by the message that "Excellence is the answer." Messages come from all directions: from verbal, written, broadcast, and visual media. Excellence has become a pervasive buzzword. It's become so fashionable to intone Excellence that we've begun to take the word for granted.

Many people pay little attention to "excellence" anymore. It's lost its impact. Too many have accepted substandard work and performance and called it "excellent" to suggest that they, too, are in the Excellence Game. We've heard the word so much that we assume excellence is commonplace. It is not.

Excellence has been painted and reinforced as a goal to be achieved, a Holy Grail for which we must crusade. With this attitude, we equate Excellence with Perfection. Perfection is practically unattainable, sometimes inappropriate, and often needlessly expensive. Achieving "Excellence as Perfection" is unrealistic and counterproductive for many of America's companies and their people.

Striving for Excellence May Cause Failure

In reality, Excellence is such a lofty goal that it often exceeds your vision. You aren't sure just what it is or how to recognize it when you see it. But, you know you're supposed to achieve it, so you sometimes label as "excellent" results which you know are not. You want to demonstrate that you've achieved something. This deception irritates your integrity and sense of ethics. Your conscience alarm rings annoyingly.

You set your goals, your ideals, so high, you can't possibly achieve them. In most organizations, Excellence has become a nebulous concept. "Oh, that's just something they put on posters, advertising literature, and in the annual report." It doesn't mean anything specific. Aha! We're living a lie. A sham. We're teaching our employees to lie!

When you can't achieve the level of excellence you're told to expect of yourself, you sense an internal feeling of unworthiness . . . almost dishonesty. This guilt can eat away at you, reducing your productivity, effectiveness, and self-esteem. This feeling can cause some serious internal problems, personally and organizationally.

Since you recognize that Excellence is a goal worthy of your striving, you quite naturally reach for it. You keep reaching, sometimes vigorously, higher and higher, trying to grasp it. You keep reaching, and falling short. You never really feel that you've achieved the almost undefinable state of Excellence.

The experience is much like the legendary fox leaping for the grapes. And, like the fox, you fail to grasp your goal. Excellence, for many, has become "sour grapes."

Eventually, after expending great amounts of energy, time, and money, you may lose confidence in your ability to achieve that elusive quality of Excellence. You fall back to your previous level of activity. Sometimes you fall back even further as a result of your exhaustion and frustration.

Sometimes you just give up. Or, as noted earlier, you

label what you know to be a lesser achievement as "excellent". This exercise can be self-defeating. It has been for many managers, their subordinates, and their employers. It's so easy to settle into self-deluding mediocrity.

Sometimes there is a net gain, however. Your forging forward has enabled you to make a few improvements. Occasionally, those gains remain in force as a long-lasting strength of the organization. In other cases, though, the gains evaporate for lack of reinforcement.

What's Really Happening?

A question asked by many managers and their subordinates is, "What have we gained?" They honestly know they have not achieved Excellence, so where are they? Self-doubt and a sense of inadequacy are experienced. These feelings create anxiety, depression, and become frustratingly negative to the individual and the organization.

Many organizations which have been touted as "excellent" in the past aren't really doing so well now. The anecdotes sound wonderful until you talk privately with people who work for those companies. Employees tell some outrageous stories that belie the legends. We've been fooled by "snapshots" . . . scenes that look good just as the shutter snaps, but don't really tell the whole story. Remember how cute the baby was, gurgling and grinning for the camera? Then, the second after the picture was taken, the crying tantrum started! A lot of snapshots of companies have similar stories: there are a lot of tantrums out there!

In spite of all this, we persist in preaching Excellence and following "Excellence" gurus like they were Pied Pipers. We join the cult of Excellence-worshippers. Corporations and their leaders are caught up in the fantasy. Their subordinates, reluctant to challenge The Image, follow along like obedient sheep. Remember the story of the Emperor's new clothes?

Some executives distribute current books for managers to

read, but most managers don't read them. At least not completely. If you read the popular books in the field of management and leadership, you may perceive your superiors showing inappropriate behaviors and values.

It's hard to be inspired to practice MBWA (Management by Wandering Around) when your superior doesn't leave his/her office! Can you inspire your people to be loyal and supportive when your boss acts like an ungrateful tyrant?

A Different Perspective

It's time to look at Excellence from a different perspective. It's time to be more realistic in the way we look at high performance in our personal and business lives. It's time to be more honest with ourselves and others as we consider what excellence really means to us.

In this book, you'll look at "excellence"—at high performance—from a "how-to" perspective. You'll learn about practical things you can do. You'll strive to grow and improve your performance as an individual, as a member of a work group, and as a leader. You'll look critically and realistically at the impact of your attitudes and behaviors on the people around you. What you do matters. You, and your leadership style—what you practice, not just what you preach—make a significant difference. The attitude-based deliberate actions you take to move toward "Excellence" are described as *The Process of Excelling*.

"Excelling" is an active verb. The meaning is not limited to surpassing others, but includes your surpassing your own prior performance. It means doing your best at whatever you do—in business, in your family and personal life, in your community. It's an attitude, a set of behaviors, a way of life. Excelling means never being satisfied with less than your best efforts. And best results.

In this book, you will not be smothered with examples of companies or individuals who have, in someone's view, demonstrated excellence. Your concern should not be to focus on examples of what might have been accomplished at one moment, or even over a period of time, by someone else. Instead, focus on how to help yourself and your people to excel, to reach your highest possible levels of achievement.

Each of the elements of *The Process of Excelling* carries equal weight. Every one of the techniques explored in this book will contribute to the achievement of your excelling performance. One of the most difficult tasks in putting this book together was determining the order of the chapters. Each aspect of the process is vital, so the order of the chapters is random except for the first two elements.

The first element, Sense of Direction, is the starting point for everything else you do. Clarifying Expectations follows closely behind. You'll appreciate this more as you learn about these aspects in chapters five and six.

At the conclusion of each chapter are several thought-provoking questions about the ideas that have been presented. Use these questions to stimulate your individual thought. Share the inquiry with others to stimulate discussion about how each of you is doing individually . . . and about how you're doing as a group. We've also given you a blank page at the end of each chapter to record thoughts that occur to you as you read about these different ideas. Feel free to make some notes about other things you've read or heard that relate to the techniques being explored.

This book is not a treatise about what others have done. It's an approach to what you can do. There is no question that you can reach higher levels of achievement that will make your life more satisfying and productive. All of us have room for substantial growth if we desire to make the effort.

Set an example for others to follow. Then, you and all those who work with you will use the ideas in this book to excel with pride! With this awesome power, you can really make a significant difference!

It's up to you!

1

All Hail Excellence!

"Excellence" is the answer! Let us worship Excellence! All hail Excellence!

Excellence has become a common expression in business, education, government, health care, and a variety of other environments. The word and the concept have earned the status shared by Motherhood, Apple Pie, and The Flag. To argue against Excellence is practically blasphemy! Excellence has been revered as a goal, as a target, as a state of being, as a way of life.

While we don't hear anyone knocking "excellence," the popularity of the buzz word has waned. It's become like an over-used vacation spot. Everyone knows where it is and agrees that it's wonderful, but no one wants to go there. Instead, our attention has been drawn to empowerment, re-engineering, life balance, total quality and continuous improvement, alternative life styles, and spirituality. We continue to be fascinated by the latest approach to finding a better way to live and work. We're looking for someone else to give us the answers, the easy way.

Some History

The Excellence movement grew rapidly during the 1980s and early 1990s. For a while, it almost seemed like a populist revolution. The movement was fueled by such people as "business evangelist" Tom Peters, by media reports, and by the inevitable university studies. Management consultants and other authors wrote a truckload of books dealing with Excellence, High Achievement, Peak Performance, and similar appealing topics. People grabbed anything they saw on the subject. We developed an Excellence Cult in the early 1980s that persists today.

Yes, the "excellence talk" is still in place, and that's not all bad. Wallowing in mediocrity, we needed a jolt of that achievement message. For most people and most companies, that is all it is—just talk. In the beginning, corporate mangers would buy copies of Tom Peter's seminal work, *In Search of Excellence,* to display in their offices as a sort of trophy. They didn't read it, at least not all of it, but they did display the "badge of excellence" for all to see.

It's interesting today, years after that book took the best seller lists by storm, to see so many copies of the familiar volume in used book stores, garage sales, and Goodwill Industries' shelves. Tom Peters fueled a powerful movement with his seminal work, but many managers never "bought in." They gave "lip service" to the pursuit of excellence, but didn't follow through. Other titles have since replaced *In Search of Excellence* as office trophies, the "I've read this, so you do it" attitude prevails. The commitment that Peters urged did not materialize.

The books, articles, studies, and speeches elevated many companies to near-sainthood because of their perceived high levels of achievement. Some "excellent" companies were cited repeatedly in Peters work and other publications, while others just received an occasional mention. A handful of companies basked in the enhanced reputation they gained from the praise being heaped on them by the Excellence watchers and the Baldridge Award program. Their corporate recruiters were no doubt appreciative of the image projected!

In the meantime, other companies not mentioned in the literature were also achieving high levels of performance. Some of their leaders publicized these accomplishments through speeches, display advertising, and promotional events at trade shows. Others concentrated their focus on strong communication with their customers and prospective customers. Some said little about their attainments—just getting the job done without a particular need to toot their horns.

Thumb through a few popular and business magazines to see advertisements promoting company excellence. Years after the initial popularity of the "excellence" descriptor, the term is still used in market positioning by many employers— seeking good customers, employees, and investors. Other companies are quietly effective, proving themselves through performance without ballyhoo or flamboyance. Their strength is reflected in comments made by their customers and industry observers.

After we raised corporations onto their pedestals, we began to elevate their leaders to similar positions of reverence. It wasn't long before we discovered we had some false gods in our worship of Excellence. The sacred cows began to melt under the heat of scrutiny. We started questioning the hype.

Our attention was drawn back to "excellence" as a philosophy, as a way of life.

Still not satisfied with "excellence" for its own sake, we kept searching for the easy answers. It was like we were looking for a pill to take to make it all better—to make mediocrity go away, to inspire everyone to do his/her best.

Following on the heels of the Excellence push, we placed a great deal of emphasis on total quality management (TQM). This concept became a popular bandwagon, with all sorts of corporations and their leaders trumpeting the coveted benefits of program after program. The "me too" syn-

drome appeared again. These were prosperous times for consultants, printers, and banner makers. In the short run, we
saw some improvements and we realized (again) that we
could achieve at higher levels than we had been.

Enlightened companies eventually moved away from the
programmatic aspects of quality improvement, choosing
instead just to concentrate on sharing ideas, actions, and dedication to continuous improvement. They found that the struc-
tures weren't necessary; we don't need more committees,
meetings to go to, and reports to write. Let's just get it done!

This irritation and frustration with the TQM formalities
and competition caused us to examine more carefully what's
really needed to build performance, results, and pride.

Aha! It's people working together. In rolled the bandwagon marked "team leadership."

We rode that wagon around the parade field for a while
until we realized that we didn't need to formalize team leadership and call attention to it. Team leadership, collaboration,
sharing of visions and results should be a natural aspect of
how people work together.

Well, if teaming isn't the whole answer, perhaps we ought
to encourage people to work on their own. Let's give them a
sense of power to make their own decisions and to get things
done without running to someone else for approval. This
movement was like the clown car charging into the center
ring of the management circus. One after another, the
empowerment ideas came bouncing out of the car. Individual
Initiative! Creativity! Accountability! Solo Decision Making!

Maybe the answer is re-engineering. Or principle-cen-
tered leadership. Or some other fad-of-the-month. Everyone
wants to come up with his or her own idea of the management principle that will save the world. Silly. This isn't brain
surgery or rocket science. We're simply re-packaging the
same stuff.

There's nothing new in management or leadership. These
are the same concepts we've been talking about for years!

Management writers make the simple more elaborate or restate the obvious. Take off the window dressing and we return to the same basic foundation.

From my perspective, it makes more sense to go back to the fundamentals that were presented in the first edition of this book 'way back in 1988 (and they'd been around for a long time before I talked about them in the seminars that spawned this book). We keep looking for answers that have been right in front of us all the time!

Unfortunately, a lot of people just can't see the answers. They can't appreciate the simplicity of high performance, of high achievement. Watch what happens around you. Read the magazines, trade journals, and newspapers. You'll hear more about corporate re-engineering until we get bored with that bright idea and search for another. It's been quite a parade and, unfortunately, it will continue. Let's look for the simple answers, the fundamentals that enable us to excel—as individuals, as teams, and as organizations.

Even with the continuing fad-like approaches to management improvement, numerous corporate executives continue to promote the fundamental concept of excellence within their organizations through newsletters, posters, employee meetings, and person-to-person contact. The "word" is still heard as a rallying cry in many work environments. The concept of "excellence" remains central to the operating philosophies in a wide range of businesses in the United States and in other countries. It doesn't much matter what we call it, as long as our motives are sincere.

Understandably, in many manufacturing companies, the message is that we must excel to compete with foreign manufacturers. An increasing number of domestic companies are tired of the foreign incursion and actively seek ways to fight back. While the weapons they use include trade quotas and multinational corporate relationships, the most successful tools are how well how they work with their people. Our human resources are our most valuable resources. We need to place our emphasis on people—in both individual and group perspectives.

Interestingly, the domestic companies that feel threatened are returning to the methods the foreigners "borrowed" from corporate America to achieve their own success. A generation or two ago, representatives of foreign companies were studying how Americans ran their companies. They successfully copied and used our approaches while we tried new ideas. For example, many of the methods identified with Japanese companies were learned from the late W. Edward's Deming, an American citizen.

Beyond the Corporate Walls

The focus on Excellence is not limited to the corporate environment. A number of authors and public speakers, including Charles Graveled, Denies Whitely, Joe Charbonneau, Stephen Covey, and Ken Blanchard beat the drums for individual high performance. Everyone wants to be identified with a concept like excellence, that can't be disputed and is alive with possibilities.

Public school systems are focusing on Excellence, belatedly spurred on by federal, state, and local government and civic leaders representing Americans tired of seeing less-than-adequate performance from self-serving local systems. Finally, academic needs are beginning to receive as much, or more, emphasis than athletics. Schools are demonstrably striving for higher academic achievement, competing in more arenas than just organized physical sports.

Across the country, school boards are demanding teacher competency, an attitude of dedication, and classroom performance that produces students better equipped to achieve after graduation. There is a renewed emphasis on academic achievement. Concern for academic performance never went away, but it now gets considerably more attention. Once again, high performance in education is a desirable societal goal.

Local government agencies have been plagued with the image of mediocrity. The misimpression is that people work for state and local governments because they "can't get real jobs." We've all heard the horrible expression, "it's good enough for government work." In reality, some top-flight local governments across the country are emphasizing high performance and have achieved admirable successes. They're concentrating on management training, higher levels of worker competency, innovation, and cost reduction in providing service to their communities. Even in the public sector, these exemplary governments refer to their departments as "business units."

Some agencies in America's federal government system promote Excellence. Most visible in the promotional arena has been the U.S. Postal Service. Their message is flashed to the public through a variety of media, including tractor-trailers serving as rolling billboards attesting to the alleged excellence of the express mail service. Unfortunately, excellence in the highly visible postal system has been as elusive as it has been in so many other organizations throughout the country and the world. They accomplish much, but fall far short of the standards desired by their customers. Their performance shortfall opened the door to a whole new industry: overnight courier services.

As consumers, we are becoming less tolerant of poor performance. Each of us is holding ourselves to a higher standard, and we expect the same of the organizations we patronize. Our demand for quality, service, and value will continue to increase, placing more pressure on organizations to excel in what they do. The underlying desire is there in all of us to do better in everything we do. We simply need to learn how, get focused, and gradually improve our performance, satisfaction, and price.

We'll become less satisfied with mediocrity, with complacency. In almost all aspects of our lives, we'll see that we do indeed have alternatives. We will consciously begin to make more choices. The choices will come in our personal lives, our family lives, and our work lives.

In this era, we have discovered and embraced our ability to set our standards higher (or differently), take control of our lives, our destiny, and move forward in new directions. As we seek fresh paths, and the shifts won't all be easy. Some will be painful, some will be exciting. Some changes will be easy to make, some will be very difficult. But we will make changes. We will take control of our lives. We will manage ourselves more deliberately, to be "at choice" rather than reactive to what happens to us. Each of us will seek to manage ourselves to excel in what we choose to do.

Singing the Popular Song

Public speakers, authors, trainers, consultants and even broadcast media personalities sing the song of Excellence. In various forms, it's a popular theme. People want to be better than they are. Many believe they can improve their performance by listening to examples of what others have done, and by copying their approach.

Even the companies that design and market educational programs have developed training packages that purport to teach people how to be Excellent. Executives of all kinds of organizations purchase these support services. They buy best-selling motivational books and distribute them to all their management people. "Read this book," they urge. "We're going to start doing this beginning on Monday morning." Of course, this process won't work if the leaders don't participate and set the example, set the pace. "We" means all of us, not just the rest of you.

Our bookstores and libraries are stocked with an abundance of books on how to be a high achiever—from Charles Garfield's peak performance concepts to Robert Schuller's emphasis on attitudes, Stephen Covey's focus on principles, Ray Pelletier's *Permission to Win,* and Tony Robbins' highly promoted work on personal motivation. Self-improvement books, magazines, and tapes sell well. The motivational rallies—theatres full of people listening to a parade of inspirational speakers—are back.

Some observers believe that the "self-help" attitude we saw a generation ago has returned to America. We're even seeing radio stations and television networks, such as The People's Television Network, concentrate on this movement toward individual and group improvement. Expect to see more of this; we're hungry for personal self-improvement—for its intrinsic value as well as its benefit to our careers and employers.

This self-improvement attitude has already reached beyond the individual level into the corporate context. There is an increasing desire for genuine organizational self-improvement. People want to make their companies, associations, schools, and governments more effective, more efficient, more productive, more fulfilling. The problem we face is that most front-line managers and supervisors simply don't know how to achieve that "self-improvement"—for themselves or their teams.

We seem to be reaching for that elusive something we call "Excellence," without fully knowing what it is. Each of us approaches the goal in a slightly different way, but we are reaching. It's a proud song to sing today, as we strive to be the best we can be. That striving for high personal and corporate achievement can be called "excelling."

In this book, we'll explore the twelve elements of excelling and how to apply them in your work life and your personal life. You can do this quietly, or you can strive to get others enthused to join with you in the effort. We'll still hear the "excellence" theme promoted and, you know, that's all right. We need to keep the ideal in front of us.

Our Response

Response to the call to excellence varies widely from person to person, from organization to organization. Some people ignore the concept, but continue to do the best they can in their own way. They don't get involved in the game of identifying their efforts as "excellent." They defy measurement, preferring to simply "do."

Others give lip service to the idea. They don't really do anything special, but tell others that they support and apply the concept. They ignore the need for personal involvement. This behavior is akin to the Emperor's new clothes; no one wants to proclaim that it's really not so, even though everyone knows it. Thousands of people and organizations *think* they're excellent, but they actually fall far short of that coveted standing. If you talk seriously with these people, they soon admit that they aren't really performing to their highest potential.

There are a number of bright spots. Enlightened organizations throughout the country are finding ways to advocate the concept of authentic excellence in their workplace. With suggestion programs, employee recognition activities, and other approaches, they endeavor to make it easy and comfortable for people to achieve at higher levels. The comfort is often a psychological comfort, since most workers are concerned with peer reactions, as well as what the boss thinks.

Our objective must be to make striving for high performance an accepted behavior, an endorsed behavior, something to be respected rather than scorned. It's a cultural issue—corporate culture and societal culture. When a society accepts less than the best, its institutions and people accept less than the best. Positive change is certainly possible, but it takes a concerted effort. It's a maddeningly slow process. When you want to make major shifts quickly, it's sometimes hard to remember that we've built our old habits over many years. Changing habits doesn't come easily; the old ways are deeply entrenched.

Teaching People to Excel

Discovering that many of their workers simply don't know how to perform their jobs at high performance, companies institute training programs to teach people how to do their individual jobs better. The training focuses on competency, with occasional attention to initiative, accountability, and attitude. The emphasis is on task accomplishment.

Training and retraining programs strengthen workers' abilities to perform the tasks assigned to them. Some companies use more experienced workers to teach newer employees how jobs can be done effectively, efficiently, and correctly. Vocational, trade, and technical schools are utilized to teach the skills that workers have not yet learned well.

There is a renewed interest among corporations to engage outside professionals in human resource development to improve employee performance—from the most seasoned executive to the newest hourly worker. During the late 1980s and early 1990s, numerous corporate training departments were gutted in cost-cutting moves, leaving companies without the ability to strengthen the capacity of their workforces. Bringing in outside trainers is the best option for many of these employers. Others are rebuilding their internal training departments . . . and even still using outside professional support to supplement or guide.

More and more innovative approaches will help people learn needed skills. In some cases, the teachers come to the workplace; in other cases, the employees go to outside educational facilities. Internal training programs are focusing more and more on assuring that production workers know how to perform well the tasks expected of them.

Through Statistical Process Control (SPC) and other programs, production workers are learning how to measure their own performance, to judge their own work. SPC is a system whereby industrial production workers can measure their personal performance against established statistical standards.

They know right away whether their work meets expectations, so they can make the necessary corrections on the spot. The principles have been applied in a wide variety of fields, including healthcare.

These programs build stronger accountability at progressively lower levels in the organization. Quality is emphasized, as well as quantity of output. Workers are being told, for the first time in some companies, to make sure their tasks have been done right before sending processed parts or papers on to the next work station.

This is a significant change in attitude, in the messages being received by workers from management. While we still hear the emphasis on getting work out the door (number quotas), the quality message is getting louder and louder. In some companies, production workers are told when orders have to be shipped, enabling them to join cooperatively in the effort to ship on time.

Our assembly line process has often focused worker attention on one small part of the job, instead of on the end product. Recognizing this inappropriate focus as a deficiency, enlightened companies are helping employees to understand how their individual efforts contribute to the whole. Assembly line workers are learning more and more about what happens in the rest of the plant and what the end product looks like. They are discovering the importance of their daily responsibilities to the overall results the company is trying to achieve.

Attitude and management skill training has been a back-to-basics experience in most organizations. We've realized that many managers have been appointed and anointed. When a position in supervision has opened, we've sought the best person to move up into that new position. Too often management selects the person who's been around the longest, or who has caused the least difficulty ("keeps his nose clean")—without regard to how competent that person may be as a manager or leader.

The next step in the promotion process is ceremonial. We bring these hapless soul into the inner office, on the sacred carpet, and perform a brief ritual. We mythically wave the magic wand, sprinkle some magic dust, and "poof!" Presto! We have a new supervisor, manager, executive . . . whatever. The process is the same . . . of anointment.

With no real training in how to be managers—how to perform their new roles, they've been given new responsibility without quite knowing how to get their jobs accomplished. Simply telling someone, "now you're a supervisor," does not equip that person to perform the new job.

Over the years, managers have been promoted to progressively higher positions without ever learning how to manage. They need to be educated in the theory and principles of management, the techniques to apply, and ways to most effectively manage in today's environment. An increasing number of companies are providing fundamental supervisory training for their management people, including executives in some cases. There is a lot of remedial work to be done. Too many managers are being led by people who never really learned how to manage themselves.

Successful companies emphasize the how-to approach. Employees are shown the methods to accomplish what is expected of them. Motivational programs are still there, and always will be, but now these programs are oriented toward the skills and techniques necessary to get the job done.

Training is conducted by in-house professional training staffs and by experienced employees taught to be trainers. Professional trainers are increasingly brought in as outside contractors. Technical and supervisory training programs are offered at community colleges and universities. Trade associations are becoming more involved in education for employees, managers, executives, and even company owners. We'll see more of this learning emphasis in the years ahead, often using some of the emerging technologies that make education and training available to anyone, anywhere, anytime.

Some training is being done simply because it's "the right thing to do." Training resources should be focused on helping people achieve identified personal and organizational objectives. Training can make a real difference, but it's not a cure-all. Before launching a training program, pause to determine your specific needs: what do you want the training to accomplish for you? Evaluate what you want the end results to be, so you can better design the learning steps that will take you down your chosen path.

Training and education programs should be carefully designed to help people gain the knowledge, skills, and attitudes/perspectives that will increase their chances of goal achievement. Learning can be accomplished through employer-sponsored programs, but more and more individuals will seek growth opportunities on their own.

Individual workers seeking to excel will assume their own responsibility to learn, regardless of what their current employer has to offer. We'll talk some more about approaches to learning later in this book.

There is a prevalent feeling that we need to make changes to improve our performance. Response to this feeling varies considerably from organization to organization. The effectiveness of the response efforts is also quite different. The message is being communicated, but many people hearing about Excellence aren't sure what to do or how to do it. They want the results of the change, but are often less-than-enthusiastic about going through the process.

I relate this very real feeling of discomfort and impatience to a quote attributed to Robert Louis Stevenson. When asked if he enjoyed writing, Stevenson replied, "I do not like to write, but I like to have written." This emotion is not an uncommon.

Listening to managers and supervisors across the country, in all kinds of organizations, I hear the same message. Everyone wants practical ideas that can be applied immediately to strengthen results. Managers and supervisors everywhere exclaim "It's time to move past the pretty pictures and get the job done!"

Thought-Provoking Questions

1. How have you heard the "Excellence" message? How legitimate are these examples?
2. What other books have you read that encourage high performance? What similarities or differences do you see in them?
3. What training is being done in your organization? How effective is it? How do you know?
4. How concerned are you about excelling in your personal life—really doing well practically everything you do? How has this worked for you? Does your attitude about your personal standards, your personal achievement, find its way into your work life?
5. What gets in your way of doing an absolutely fantastic job?

Reader's Notes

2

Breaking Away
from Mediocrity

Moving from mediocrity toward Excellence is not easy, *but it can be done!* And the rewards are wonderful!

Here's our predicament: the habits and tolerances of mediocrity are well-ingrained. They're part of our society, our work, our personal lives, We have accepted complacency as a way of life. We tolerate less-than-the-best, in others and in ourselves.

Mediocrity has become a societal sickness that must be cured!

How do we cure the disease? Each of us accepts responsibility to banish mediocrity from our lives. Draw the lines. You. Me. Our friends, family, co-workers, colleagues. It's up to each of us to break out of this old pattern, *to declare that we simply won't tolerate mediocrity in our lives anymore.*

But, like I said, this shift won't be easy. If it was easy, we all would have done it a long time ago. No, it's a challenge. But, those who meet the challenge quickly discover tremendous opportunities for themselves—in all aspects of their lives. The powerful sense of pride and serenity and confidence is hard to describe. But it's there . . . and it's great!

Personal and organizational high achievement can be accomplished to be sure, but it will take time. You'll need both patience and persistence. We're surrounded by negative influences that must be overcome.

To put our situation in perspective, let's compare our performance to climbing a mountain. Far below us, at the foot of the mountain, is poor performance. People laboring in the Foothills of Poor Performance are well-satisfied with their substandard work. They have practically no motivation to expend effort on improving their performance. Some even avoid work whenever possible. Most of them aren't aware that there's anything different out there. This mediocrity is all they've seen, so they think it's good. These people simply "attend work." They show up, do what they're told, and go home.

As we climb out of these depths of despair, the air becomes fresher and easier to breathe. We begin to feel a sense of accomplishment in our work. It may not be tremendously satisfying, but we're doing something positive. We are involved in some sort of productive activity. As we climb higher on the Mountain of Achievement, we feel a rise in our self-esteem. We know we're better than we were, and we begin to wonder if there's something more "up there."

As we continue our climb up the mountain of performance, a significant number of people, often through no fault of their own, settle on the Plateau of Mediocrity. When we reach that point in our climb, we feel comfortable. We can breathe more easily and enjoy a pleasant view. We know there's more mountain to climb, but don't have the motivation to invest more energy in continuing the climbing effort. We're content. Complacent.

At the top of the mountain is the peak, which we'll call "Excellence". The peak is hidden from our view by clouds. We know it's up there, but we aren't sure how far it is, what it looks like, or how we'll know when we've arrived. Our joy, our thrill, becomes the climb itself. Going higher and higher is exciting and stimulating. We know we're getting better, experiencing more, going beyond where we ever believed we could go. Every step is an intrinsic encouragement for the next.

In this example, our climb is called "excelling." It's the concentration on the upward climb. It's our experience climbing up from the Plateau of Mediocrity towards the Peak of Excellence. Excelling is not a specific achievement; it is action. "Excel" is an active verb. We're doing something.

When we're excelling, we may not be exactly sure where we are on the mountain, but we do know that we're beyond the level of mediocrity. Even if we never reach the peak, the view is much better the higher we go. There's a definite feeling of exhilaration in knowing how far we've come, and knowing that we're still climbing!

We don't climb alone. Mountain climbing experts will tell you how foolish that is. There are others climbing with us (teamwork). We reach down to help others climb along with us (mentoring). We're really not worried about falling (attitude); we're using safety equipment as recommended (planning, goal setting with alternatives, contingency plans).

All of us who are climbing know where the others are. We know what we can expect from each other in terms of support and coordination (expectations). We know what we must do for ourselves, as well as for others (initiative, responsibility, accountability). We praise each other as we reach new heights (recognition), and encourage each other to keep climbing even when the going gets rough (inspiration, support). We're all working together (support groups, caring, love) to excel at what we are doing.

We're not concerned about the mountaintop itself. Our

attention and energy is focused on our climb. We give careful consideration to where we are now and where we're going next. We concentrate on maintaining our control and perspective. In actual mountain-climbing, loss of control or perspective could be fatal.

Climbing our own mountains of achievement—personally or in our work setting, we focus on control and perspective. The same sort of threats we find in mountain climbing and similar adventures are also found in our personal and business lives. We can allow these threats to consume us, and have a very short climb. Or we can work aggressively to overcome the threats, to remove those obstacles that get in our way, and enjoy a long climb with excitement and elation with practically every step.

With the challenges of a rapidly changing world, it is imperative that we strive to excel—to do our best—in everything we do. We must make that commitment personally, professionally, and organizationally if we are to succeed. Those who fail to make that commitment probably won't succeed. They'll lead a disappointing and unsatisfying life. In fact, they may not even survive. And clearly, it's their choice.

You also have a choice. You've already begun to make that choice clearly, or you wouldn't be reading this book!

You have the knowledge and the ability to excel—for yourself, for your team, and for your employer. All you have to do now is commit. Dedicate yourself to using all your personal and organizational resources to achieve the highest possible level of performance and achievement.

In the pages that follow, I'll show you the principles that have helped thousands of high achievers accomplish so much. You'll gain the insights and inspiration to combine with your knowledge and ability. The next move is yours.

It's Attitude . . . and Choice

To develop excelling attitudes and behaviors, you have to

consistently emphasize high performance instead of the "get by" attitude. It's easier to do for yourself, but usually more difficult to accomplish with others. This shift is something each of us has to do on our own; you can't do it for anyone else. You can help them, teach them, inspire them, encourage and reinforce them; but you can't do it for them.

An important point: Each of us chooses to excel . . . or not. It's a personal choice. If a friend or someone working with you chooses not to excel, it's their choice. You will probably feel badly that they are not achieving as well as you are. It's OK to sympathize, perhaps even empathize, with their attitude and behavior. But, remember, it's their choice.

When I coach corporate executives on how they work with their employees, there is always sadness when someone has to be disciplined or discharged. I counsel them to appreciate that those employees made their own choices. If you've equipped them to perform, as we'll discuss in this book—given them the tools they need to excel, don't fault yourself if they choose not to do their best. They've made their choice, with full knowledge of the consequences. It's your job to follow through and reward them with the consequences they chose.

As you work to move others to climb their mountains, don't expect overnight results. This shift from "it's good enough" to conscious high achievement is an educational process that will happen gradually. The mediocrity attitude has been established over many years. Mediocrity is continually reinforced in our society, in spite of all the talk about excellence. Life experiences, even television shows, preach the "get by" and "get away with something" attitudes.

Yes, you'll find it easier to change your personal attitudes than those of your co-workers. Being motivated enough to read this book, you are already seeking to improve your performance, your happiness, your lifestyle. That inner drive will be enable you to better understand the value and critical importance of breaking the bonds of mediocrity. Others may not yet have your perspective, and may be less than whole-heartedly supportive of your efforts. Expect this resistance, this reluctance, and your mission will be easier to undertake.

It won't be easy. Excelling is something you must want to do.

Understanding the Enemy

It's easy to identify mediocrity as our enemy, but the problem goes deeper than that. Underlying our society's acceptance of mediocrity is a social value system. Those values, while they may not blatantly support mediocrity, also don't fight it. Mediocrity permeates our society in several forms.

First, as a culture, we have become tolerant of substandard performance, products, and services. You may not like this situation, but most people generally haven't seen any other choice. Those protesting often feel like a "lone voice in the wilderness," crying out with no one listening or lending support.

Second, striving for peak performance, for high achievement, has not been recognized and rewarded in many areas of our society. A system of protectionism has been developed, allowing people to get by with doing less than their best. That system is part of the enemy you are fighting.

A third problem we face in trying to break away from mediocrity is inertia, a force that has to be overcome to get something moving. We're striving to somehow get people to move themselves out of a rut that has become very comfortable for them. An appropriate definition of a rut comes to mind: "a grave with both ends missing." This description certainly has negative connotations; not all ruts are dysfunctional.

It is easy to get into ruts in our lives. The paths we trod are worn down with each trip we make along the same route. For better or worse, we all find ourselves in ruts that have gotten so deep, we don't recognize we're in them! Sometimes these ruts—these patterns of living—are good paths to follow. Regardless of their value, wisdom, or appropriateness, it's important to know that we are in ruts . . . our accustomed ways of doing things in our lives. That perspective is vital to our understanding of who we are, what we do, and why we do these things.

In spite of tolerance, protectionism, and inertia, you have to help yourself and your people appreciate—and be proud of—the difference between mediocrity and excelling. It's vital to understand the forces at work in each of these areas of concern, so you can appreciate what you have to overcome. Let's look a little deeper.

Tolerance of Mediocrity

As a society, we have come to accept less than the best. We have sent clear messages that substandard performance is satisfactory. Evidence of this tolerance is all around us. You probably don't like what you see, but feel powerless. You may not protest much, because of the response you receive: little or nothing is done about the problem and you may even be ridiculed for having such high expectations.

One example of the change in society's expectations is the way your car or truck is fueled and maintained. "Service station" is a misnomer. Precious few gasoline stations emphasize service today. Stations that go beyond pumping your gas for you at the "full service" island are uncommon. Remember when attendants used to check oil, tire pressure, and engine fluids? They cheerfully washed windshields, and even headlights and taillights! Stations that perform those services today earn your respect, appreciation, and customer loyalty. You reward them for moving beyond mediocrity into more excelling performance by giving them more business and telling others how pleased you are.

Even with your desire for better treatment as a customer, you observe that mediocrity is tolerated nearly everywhere you go. Even the companies classified as "service industries" really aren't, at least not to the degree that you would recognize as excelling. And you tolerate this. You simply resign yourself to using substandard products, accepting service that doesn't quite measure up, and accepting work environments that don't really seem interested in your best efforts.

Another example. How often have you walked into a retail establishment, perhaps for the first time, looking for a product that would normally be sold at this kind of store? You aren't sure where your desired merchandise is in this particular store, so you decide to ask for help. Hmmm. Lights on. Doors open. Where are the people to help you?

Finally, you find an employee and ask for what you want. What's the typical response? "Oh, it's over there in such-and-such section." "Try aisle 3." "I don't know; ask someone else." "It's not my department." Or the response that amazes me—and I've actually heard it three times—"I'm on break now." It's amazing that anyone in a customer service role would allow a break to get in the way of serving the customer. Sure, we need our breaks, but if you're in view of the customer, you're on duty as far as that customer is concerned! Mediocrity is prevalent in our society today.

Do you get the feeling that something should be done about all this? Do you wish that someone would take some kind of corrective action? Can't someone stand up for doing things the right way?

Local, state, and federal consumer protection agencies are drastically understaffed and unable to handle the flow of complaints received. As a result, they do only what they can. Dedicated problem solvers often "cave in" under the workload, doing what they can here and there and becoming increasingly frustrated with their inability to make enough of a difference.

Each of us can make a difference by speaking out when we encounter mediocrity. And, of course, we can exert a powerful influence by not allowing mediocrity to infect the way we do things in our own lives.

Protectionism

Over the past couple of generations, our society has developed an attitude and a system of protecting the under-achiever. The most blatant examples in the workplace are the civil service system, the organized labor movement, and the tradition of tenure for university faculty. Along with these most noticeable examples is the rampant endorsement of substandard performance exercised by supervisors who abdicate their responsibility to coach or discipline their subordinates. This is not to say that these examples have made no positive contributions and should be abolished. But, here's what has happened.

The civil service system in government agencies has protected employees from arbitrary termination as influential politicians move in and out of office. However, at the same time, the system has made it practically impossible to remove low producers and non-producers from their positions. People around them who want to excel become frustrated; they either adopt the institutionalized mediocre behavior, leave the system, or build tremendous stress fighting the system.

Labor unions were formed to protect workers from unfair management practices. As the years have passed, the unions have protected some workers from much-deserved discipline or termination. Contract provisions sometimes allow union members to get away with doing less than their best, condoning a lower level of achievement. Members trying to do better often encounter strong negative peer pressure. These attitudes are gradually changing as union leaders begin to work more cooperatively with management to save plants and jobs. Everyone benefits when both union and management leaders work together to encourage people to excel . . . to work at their highest level of ability.

Even the ivory towers of academia have not escaped the protection of mediocre performance. After a professor has been on the faculty long enough, an institution may grant tenure. That, in effect, is job security; the professor can not be removed from his/her position unless there is an extremely serious infraction of the rules. Under this system, we have seen professors become lazy, doing less and less for their students. Their substandard performance is tolerated because they have tenure. This creates negative feelings from other faculty members, administrators, and students.

Another protectionist system worth mentioning is our country's welfare system. In a sense, our government pays people not to work. In some cases, there is a legitimate need for governmental assistance. But, there are also many flagrant misuses of the system. When a person can "earn" more money by not working than by investing energy in an honest job, something is wrong with the system. The concept of "workfare" is well worth considering. Under this approach, work-eligible welfare recipients are required to devote a certain number of hours to public service work before they can receive their checks. While this isn't the total answer, it's a step in the right direction. This shift, already beginning in many parts of the country, will be a substantial positive influence. Gradually, we must move more people from the welfare rolls to the tax rolls.

Supervisors who let "good enough" pass send a clear message, a message that is directly counter to the building of an excelling organization. When children do something wrong, they expect to be disciplined by their parents or other responsible adults. Child psychologists tell us that some kids actually misbehave to get attention; they know they can count on a response when they get out of line. If they don't get the discipline they expect, they view the lack of action as a lack of love.

Adults are kids in bigger bodies. We know that we take a risk when we violate the rules or don't live up to the established standards. If we don't get attention from those responsible, we perceive a lack of love—or caring. And if the boss doesn't care, why should we?

The danger here is actually on two levels. If the poor performer is not brought up to standard or disciplined, that worker will not meet expectations. All sorts of performance problems result from that circumstance. Going further, let's recognize that the other workers know full well that the substandard performance is being ignored— accepted. They assume the boss is happy with (or actually wants) lower performance, so they accommodate. Those workers who don't want to lower their own personal standards quit to take jobs where their high achievement is desired and appreciated. Imagine what caliber of worker remains behind.

Initiating the Change

Part of our culture says do what you have to do, period. "I put in my eight hours" is a familiar expression. Compensation programs, incentive and reward systems, and management attitudes serve in many cases to discourage people from "going that extra mile". This has to change. Now is the time to shift your culture, our society's culture, to one of high achievement, not minimal accomplishment.

Your first initiative should be to work with individuals to inspire greater dedication and productivity. Coach each person personally, removing whatever obstacles are in the way and providing needed training, skill development, and encouragement. As the members of your team adopt the high achievement attitude and performance, they will form like-minded groups or teams within the work organization. As people begin collaborating more and more for high achievement, you will see beautiful results. Why? Simple. These folks will do better because they want to, not because they have to.

This won't be easy, since your employees will receive negative reinforcement from a variety of sources inside and outside the workplace. You'll need to counteract the negatives, most of which you have no control over, by infusing the work environment with as many positive statements, encouragements, reinforcements as you can.

The systems can be changed, but it can be a long, slow process. Gradually, the level of fabricated protection can be reduced. Unfortunately, you can't wait for all those changes to occur naturally. Your mission is to do something now to make a difference.

Encourage yourself and your people to strive for higher achievement, individually and as a team. Seeing the results of that powerful effort will build a greater sense of self-value . . . enhanced self-esteem. The real key is to motivate individuals to strive for greater personal results, building on the force of their own self-esteem. Your opportunity lies in unlocking the talents and desires your people already have within them.

You have the power—and the obligation—to positively influence individuals. Systems don't improve unless people invest conscious efforts to make them work better. Self-motivated individuals, joining deliberately together in teams, can decisively move organizations from mediocrity to higher levels of achievement. The results can be dramatic!.

As you manage your own personal high achievement, engage in the powerful practice of positive self-talk. I am a firm believer that we can manage ourselves, the same way we can manage others. We are our own managers. Become your own inspiration.

Find other high achievers to use as examples for yourself. You are your own best friend.

Inertia

Overcoming inertia to break people away from mediocrity will be difficult. People are influenced in many ways to simply remain the way they are. Why get better? No one really cares. The message is pounded home by a wide variety of signals in our society. Among these influences is the culture of the work organizations in which we function. Peer pressure and the perceived attitude of your fellow managers and supervisors must be recognized.

Mediocrity, acceptance of less than the best, is communicated to you and your people early in life. Some of this attitude is learned at home, then reinforced in school.

Remember, when you were a child, how your parent(s) would come home from work. What messages did you hear? "Wow! What a great day! I sure accomplished a lot. I can't wait to go back to work tomorrow. This is great. I love my job!" Very few of us heard that kind of attitude from our parents. The messages we did hear influenced our attitude toward work, at least initially. Food for thought: what messages do you convey to your children about work, excelling, high performance, personal achievement?

The mediocrity message comes pounding it like the surf on a beach through the broadcast and print media. In addition to the kind of stories we hear on the news programs, the entertainment shows are often negative toward work and high achievement. These shows may be fun and funny, but the subtle messages do very little to encourage excelling attitudes and performance. You see the mediocrity message everywhere. This continual reinforcement results in low motivation for you to do the best in whatever you do.

People generally don't pay enough attention to details that spell the difference between high performance and "it's OK that way." There are many examples of less-than-our-best performance. When you become sensitive to it, you'll observe mediocrity everywhere you go. As you become more sensitized to the subconscious messages in our lives, you'll be better equipped to defend yourself—and others—against the barrage.

Break the Mediocrity Cycle

To break away from mediocrity, concentrate on excelling

. . . on doing your best. "Best" will be different for each of us, but if each of your people does his or her best, imagine the change you'll see! Most people admit readily that they aren't doing their best, that they're not performing at their full potential. Amazingly, many we've surveyed perceive the supervisor's attitude and behavior to be the principal blockage to their own high performance.

I doubt that many of us ask our people not to work so hard . . . "you'll make me look bad if you produce too much." But that's a message workers often get—inadvertently. You see, if we're not emphasizing positive messages, people automatically assume the negative. There is no neutral. The technique: continually emphasize the positive in all you do with yourself and others.

Working with your subordinates and co-workers, you can help break the cycle of mediocrity. First, dedicate yourself to doing your best. Set an example for others to see and follow, and don't be satisfied with less than your best. Second, don't be satisfied with less than the best from your people. Explain to others that you expect their top performance. Enlist their support in breaking away from mediocrity. Third, be patient and persistent. Remember that permanent significant change doesn't happen overnight.

Be alert for positive achievements by your people, by other people, and by organizations with which you interact. Recognize those achievements with praise and sincere appreciation.

As more and more people become dedicated to excelling, you will gradually see less and less mediocrity. It's a process that happens one person at a time. Your results may not be perfect, but just moving in the right direction will make a noticeable difference.

As your people and your organization practice excelling more and more, you will see some gratifying results. Take pride in your achievements! Share your pride with everyone who has made your excelling performance possible—your co-workers, suppliers, customers, and others. Thank them for their contributions, and offer ways to help them improve their performance in whatever they are doing.

Share your energy to light another's candle.

Excelling will become a new way of living, of working. It's a phenomenon that has to be nurtured and reinforced. If not maintained, excelling behaviors can slip back to complacency, to mediocrity. Your support of excelling performance must be continual.

You must consciously break away from mediocrity to become the high achiever you can be. Commit yourself to always do your best, regardless of what you are doing. Never again be satisfied with less than your best.

Thought-Provoking Questions

1. What examples of mediocrity have you seen recently? How did you feel about them?
2. What influence do you have over the quality of service you receive? How often do you exercise that influence, and what are the results?
3. How can you deliberately move yourself, and others, away from mediocrity?
4. What are you doing to stamp out mediocrity in your life?

Reader's Notes

3

Personal and Team High Performance

High performance is a behavior, a way of living. It's based on a strong, positive attitude. Combined with that attitude is the discipline to apply one's talents and abilities to get things accomplished. When both the positive attitude and the resultant behavior are supported, people can—and will—perform to the full extent of their capabilities. This performance is evident in the workplace, in social and civic organizations, in school settings, and in our personal lives.

A manager's job is to enable his/her people to perform to their maximum. You see, most people really want to do their best—on the job and in other aspects of their lives. There is a strong correlation between work and non-work lives. If our workplace values are not in congruence with our personal values, we experience stress that can have some serious negative impacts on our lives. When we manage ourselves and/or our people to perform at high levels, we're reaching deep into the high esteem that most people hold for themselves. It's a basic instinct that's too often ignored or suppressed.

In most organizations, workers are not able to achieve to their maximum capability because perceived obstacles block them from high performance. To help your people and organization excel, you must remove as many obstacles as you can. The only way you'll be able to determine what obstacles might be in the way is to (repeatedly) interview each person to discover what the perceived barriers might be.

You can do this kind of exercise with yourself, too. Sit down with a pencil and paper in a quiet place and make a list of those things that seem to be getting in your way.

Make some notes about why or how each impediment is blocking you. This discovery process will be very valuable to you: Now that you see what may be getting in your way of higher achievement, you can take steps to remove those restraints.

Unfortunately, many workers perceive their immediate supervisors, as well as upper management, as a significant part of those obstacles. They look at management as a large boulder in the middle of the stream . . . an obstacle the water has to go around to continue flowing.

Do your subordinates perceive you as an obstacle to their high performance? Unconsciously, you may be sending messages telling your people not to produce at their highest level. You probably don't intend to, but it could be happening. For instance, if you let someone get by with mediocre production on a project, other people see that. They may interpret your behavior as saying that less than the best is OK. If they want to please you—and they do consciously or subconsciously, they will produce at levels comparable to those who seem to have pleased you before.

By your action, or inaction, you train others.

Front-line supervisors and middle managers are influenced by their own perceptions of what upper management wants. Those feelings are passed along to their subordinates as easily as water flows downhill. If lower echelon managers are disgruntled by some policies or actions of upper management, those negative attitudes filter through the management ranks to poison the attitudes of the people on the front lines. All the people you're depending on to get the work done are affected.

It's difficult for lower level managers to insulate themselves from the attitudes and behaviors of their superiors. Some front line managers have been successful by focusing intently on their work group, finding ways to beat the system or work around their superiors to accomplish their own mission. This focus is why, for total success in achieving excellence, the commitment must be shared by all managers in your organization. Vertical consistency is essential. Disagreements must be worked out. The focus should be on the results to be achieved, more than the specific methods involved. The culture, the attitudes, must be mutually supportive, however.

If people perceive that your organization's leadership is satisfied with mediocre performance, that attitude becomes ingrained in the corporate culture. Unless a clear message to change that orientation is communicated and reinforced, the "low-performance- tolerated-here" perception will remain in force. It's something like seeking the lowest common denominator. In this condition of corporate atrophy, steps must be taken to continually improve or we'll naturally become progressively worse.

So, to build high performance among your subordinates, the message must come from the highest possible level in your organization. In the absence of high level support, you can still encourage your own subordinates. It won't be as easy as it would be if the entire organization were congruent. Your people will be surrounded by others who may not support your way of doing things. However, if you concentrate, you can build and maintain your own excelling team within the larger organization. The pride that comes from high achievement will help you inspire your people to excel, even when surrounded by mediocrity.

As individuals, we receive messages from a variety of people in our lives. The members of our nuclear family, our relatives, our neighbors, our friends, our contacts in the world of work all send us messages about who we are, what we do, and how well we do it.

Understandably, when you're interacting with such a large and diverse group, the messages may not be at all consistent with each other . . . or with the message you "hear" from deep within yourself.

You must decide which messages are consistent with who you are . . . and who you're striving to be. It may be necessary to make some hard choices. If you can't sufficiently insulate yourself from the inconsistent messages, from the less-than-supportive messages, you may need to make some substantial changes in your life. You alone determine who you will listen to, and how. At some point, you have to choose among alternative lifestyles . . . and take whatever steps are necessary to maintain your personal integrity.

Teamwork

We work together in teams in practically everything we do in the workplace. Rare are jobs that can be done without contact with at least one other person. In some cases, people working together function deliberately as work groups, perceiving themselves as a team. In other cases, interrelationships are more fleeting without a specific team orientation. Regardless of the strength of the bonds, we do influence each other on a regular basis.

Our work groups can be described as "partnerships," even if they're only brief encounters. Even when working together on something with one other person, a "group" exists. When the participants are working toward common goals with common values (say, excelling), we really have teams in operation.

All the people who report to you form a work group—a team. They are linked together by similar function, objectives, location, or just by the fact that they all report to you. Within that team, you have many smaller teams—some working continually together, others on merely on as-needed basis. You can bind them all together as high performers: your team. You, as their manager, as their leader, set the pace for them.

To achieve team high performance, several things have to be done. First, all members of your work group must receive your message that high performance is important to you and is expected of everyone. Second, each member of your team must invest his or her personal energies into being the best he/she can be. Third, you have to provide on a continuing basis the resources, support, and leadership to build and maintain team focus on high performance.

Excelling is not something that will happen just because you say so. It's a process you have to keep practicing, keep working on, to achieve your desired results.

As people work consciously together, a team energy is created. That energy is greater than the energy generated by the total of each of your people working independently. That team energy is called "synergy". Synergy is a power of interactive support that is positive for everyone involved.

For example, suppose three of you are stuck in a hole that is too deep to climb out of. None of you can get out. You're trapped. What's the solution here? Let's work together for our mutual benefit. If you boost one person up and out of the hole, he or she can pull another one of us up with a little boost from the one who's left. Then the two people on top can reach down and pull the third person out. You've worked together as a team to do what none of you could do alone. That's synergy.

As your team members become aware of their synergy, the

power will become even stronger for them. It will be fueled by their joint commitment to high performance, encouraged and supported by you as their leader. The team cohesiveness will build a resiliency that will resist outside challenges to the team's strength and unity. Through the process of developing synergy, trust, team-ness, and pride, you will build and enhance an excelling team and total organization.

As you support your team members in their efforts to perform to their maximum, you will be encouraging cooperation in the management of tasks, time, resources, personal energy, and communication. Your role will become more of a coordinator and support person as your team members function increasingly on their own. As you help them build their competence, their capacity and confidence will enable them to perform beautifully with minimal direction and guidance from you.

Your team will work well with you, taking advantage of the input you have from senior management and your peers, to determine clearly what is expected from the work group. Each member of the group will gain clarity of what is expected of him/her. The enriched understandings and the synergy will produce high team performance as a natural consequence. This high achievement will continue to grow as you reinforce the positive attitudes and behaviors.

Part of your job as leader of this group will be to help each of your subordinates maximize personal performance. Recognize that one person's top performance won't be the same as another's. However, in spite of their varying abilities, each person striving for high performance will make a viable contribution to the group's total performance.

The Critical Trends

Faced with increasingly rising costs, organizations are seeking ways to do more with less. The "lean machine" concept is in vogue—get the job done with the least number of people and other resources. Some argue that organizations are cutting back excessively. They say there won't be enough people to do the job without "expecting too much" of the workers.

But, the lean machine principle works. Getting rid of "dead wood" cuts costs. The total organization is strengthened as remaining high achievers are affirmed and supported. You can expect to see more application of this approach as more organizations face the reality of runaway costs, inefficiencies, and mis-allocated resources. There will be a settling out period, but eventually, most organizations will grow again . . . though probably not as big or unwieldy as they were before the "tight-sizing."

The organizations that will survive—and thrive—will be the ones that adopt the principles of excelling. You, as a manager and leader, will be challenged to maximize the productivity of your work group. You'll be expected to get the maximum possible return from your available resources.

This sought-after higher performance is possible to achieve. Your expectations of yourself and of your team will increase as you discover how much power you really have among your people. Remember that your people want to do their best. Your opportunity, your obligation, is to make it possible for them to do so by providing the environment, resources, and support they need.

Thought-Provoking Questions

1. If you aren't able to gain the cooperation of fellow managers, can you still apply the Process of Excelling in your organization? What impact(s) could you have?
2. What is the significance of working in teams?
3. Do all people really want to do their best? If not, why not? If so, how can we encourage them to demonstrate that attitude in their work environment?

Reader's Notes

4

Individual and Organizational Achievement

To excel, people must produce something of value to themselves and to others. It doesn't matter whether the end result is a product or a service or whether it is consumed by the organization itself or an outside customer. The perceived value must exist. In their work roles and their personal lives, people want to feel that they're making a contribution to their organization and to society.

Part of your responsibility as a manager and team leader is to help your people appreciate that they actually are achieving something worthwhile. Enable them to see that they are creating something of value, confirming the fulfillment of their need for significant task accomplishment. Your people need to know that they are making a viable contribution to the organization.

To be most effective in your efforts to verify and communicate achievement to your people, the work they perform should be measurable in some way. In a few occupations, the measurement may be more difficult than in others. However, even in the kind of work where specific numerical evaluations are difficult, try to find a way to provide a comparison against expectations.

Show legitimate validation to confirm to your team that their achievement is highly worthwhile. Whenever possible, let them know that their accomplishment is definitely not "ordinary" or mediocre, but something worthy in which you can all take pride.

You don't have to call the accomplishment "excellent"; in fact, it's probably better that you don't. Remember that the word used as a noun has a connotation of "the best." If you feel your people might do as well—or even better— in the future, you may want to describe their achievement using other words. Sometimes, if people feel they've achieved "the best," it takes the fun out of trying to be even better. Why ruin the adventure for them?

Telling people that they are excelling might be all right, but merely congratulating them on another positive achievement may be better. Consider your people and your circumstances, then make your own decision as to how to best communicate your beliefs to your team.

One of your most important responsibilities is to let your people know about their (increasingly) high achievements. That's what they're striving for, so always be sure your people know how they're doing. Set goals for yourself—actually put them down on paper.

Measure your personal achievement so you'll be keenly aware of when to congratulate yourself.

Each member who contributes to the team's achievement, even in a small way, should learn about what the whole group has accomplished. Even if the achievement isn't yet as good as it could be, you should still let your people know how they're doing. Tell people how their work is measured and perceived by others. Your team should take legitimate pride in its accomplishments. Their individual efforts, bonded together, produced a worthwhile achievement.

Each of your subordinates want to feel a sense of personal contribution to your team's success. Each should understand how his or her work contributes to the whole. Help your valuable people see how their particular piece fits into the puzzle. This kind of communication is desirable because it validates each person's participation and provides a sense of value, a sense of belonging. Engendering this personal sense of pride will serve as a motivator.

Organizational Achievement

Your people should also be proud of the achievements of the total organization, even if their work doesn't have direct impact on some of those achievements. Regardless of their place in the organization, they're still part of the aggregate team. Organizational accomplishments in various arenas should be shared with all employees.

Organizations achieve in different ways. There are a number of measurements that may be of interest to your people. Keep your employees informed about achievements in productivity, research and development, market penetration, sales volume, and even how your company is doing on the stock market (if your stock is traded publicly).

Particularly valuable is any information you can share about your organization's leadership in any field. This knowledge instills a special sense of pride that builds loyalty, a stronger team feeling, and higher performance. People who perceive high achievement in their organization will direct their personal efforts to their own high achievement. The standards for personal, team, and organizational achievement are all related. Your organizational culture should include high achievement as a taken-for-granted expectation.

Organizations achieve growth and greatness through innovation. Leadership comes from discovering new products, new markets, or new ways of doing things. Encourage innovation in your work group. Stimulate creativity wherever you can. Explore your personal opportunities for creativity and innovation. What can you do differently that will make you even more unique, may open new doors, or just give you a good feeling about having done something special?

Innovation comes from experimentation, which involves risk. To reach high levels of achievement, risk is necessary With risk comes the chance of failure. Not every experiment with products, markets, materials, processes, or systems is an overwhelming success. Encourage experimentation, but also give permission for people to fail if you want them to try new approaches. Take risks yourself, reaching out for the possibility of great advances in your personal position.

Granting permission to fail does not mean you expect failure. On the contrary, you should expect your people to think things through carefully enough to minimize the risk of failure. Regardless, your people need to know they have your support to move forward without fear of retribution if something doesn't work right.

As you manage yourself, continually challenge yourself about whether you are using all your capabilities to the fullest extent possible. Take some chances. Remember the turtle: he never makes any progress until he sticks his neck out.

What We Do Matters

As your team members gain more insight into how their personal effort makes a difference, you will realize greater results. They'll become better producers as they see that their team and their organization have a reputation for high achievement. They want to feel that what they do at work matters. Their achievement, no matter how small a part of the big picture, needs to have a significant impact somewhere, somehow.

People want to know that someone cares about what they do—that their effort is having an impact on someone or some part of the organization. Help your people relate what they do to what the organization does. Show them the common thread that ties everyone together.

All organizations and work teams do have one thing in common: all serve customers. Your organization provides goods and/or services to customers, clients, or patrons. Your team provides goods or services either directly to external customers or to other teams (internal customers) within your organization. An accounting department in a manufacturing firm, for instance, doesn't serve the firm's external customers directly by providing the firm's product. The accounting team does, however, serve other departments within that firm. It's their fine internal service performance that enables other departments to serve the company's external customers so well.

Regardless of the function of the individual employee or team, a strong emphasis should be placed on serving the customer. High achievement and assertive customer service are very closely linked.

By consistently and deliberately serving your customers in the best way possible, you'll demonstrate the excelling attitude and performance. Your customers will recognize and appreciate your strong interest in them; your high achievement orientation will be clearly transmitted.

Your goal should be to build strong relationships with loyal customers by being sensitive to them and by meeting their needs. Encourage everyone on your team to becustomer-oriented. The results of that thinking and behavior will contribute to everyone's high achievement.

Thought-Provoking Questions

1. Do your people feel their work has value to the organization and society? Consider ways to enhance that feeling and build job satisfaction.
2. What is your organizations position on risk-taking? Do your people really believe you want fresh ideas for improvement? How is innovation encouraged?
3. Is your emphasis on customer service strong enough? How can you intensify customer service attitude and performance?

Reader's Notes

5

A Sense of Direction

D o you sometimes wonder where you're going in life? Are you confused about where your organization is going, and what part you're expected to play in getting there?

You aren't alone. An incredible number of companies, government agencies, and non-profit organizations of all types are plagued by a lack of planning and by deficiencies in sharing what plans they do have with those responsible for getting the job done. Amazingly, these organizations continue to exist. Sooner or later many of them find themselves struggling to survive instead of striving to achieve at higher levels.

Why does this happen? Usually it's because the people responsible for setting the direction and guiding others are confused. You may fit into this category. You aren't sure where the organization is going, yet you feel you're making progress. Your position may be different than it was yesterday, but you're not sure where you're supposed to be tomorrow.

The problem is a lack of planning in all facets of the organization, particularly among the senior leaders. The result is that the organization just "floats." A popular quotation admonishes, "if you don't know where you're going, any road will take you there." That's what seems to happen. We sense movement, but aren't sure if it's in the right direction.

The lack of direction and purpose at the top affects people throughout the organization. Bewildered employees begin to compare their existence to something out of Alice in Wonderland.

Where Are We Going?

To enable an organization to excel, the first thing you must determine is the direction the organization is to take. This is described as the mission or purpose. The big question is "why are we here?" You have to define what your organization is all about. Why does it exist?

This should be Step Number One for newly-forming organizations, but the same question must be asked in organizations that have been around for quite a while. If top management has focused on the question in the past, it bears periodic re-examination. Are you still sure that's where you want to go? Is this still a legitimate statement of your mission?

In my speeches and seminars, I tell a story about the Viking explorers we learned about in our school history classes. The proud Vikings sailed the seas seeking new lands and riches. Remember the pictures we saw in our history books? The Viking captain, with his horned helmet, was shown standing proudly high in the bow, peering ahead to the future. On benches below him, rowing hard, were the hearty oarsmen. The sides of the Viking ship were high, to protect the oarsmen from attack from their enemies.

Thinking back on that scene of a working team, I can't help but ponder if the oarsmen might have ever glanced up to the bow wondering if anybody was steering. Are we headed somewhere? Or are we just meandering around the ocean? Or maybe we're still tied to the dock! Do your people know that someone is steering your vessel? Are they aware that you know where you're going?

Your mission statement establishes who you are and why you exist as an organization or as a person. It documents how you differentiate yourself from similar organizations, explaining why you are unique. The emphasis is on the reasons, the purpose, the "why" that drives you each day.

Many companies and individuals also have a vision statement. This declaration looks more specifically at how you see yourself at some point in the future—5, 10, 15 years (or whatever time frame you choose) down the road of life. With a written vision of what you hope to be, it's easier to map out the steps that will move you from where you are today to where you want to be.

Once you understand your mission or purpose and your vision, you can begin to ask yourself: to fulfill our mission, to achieve our vision, what should we be doing? In one sense, the mission is the "why"; our vision is the "what," particularly the what-we-want-to-be-in-the-future. Our next step is to examine the "how."

The "how" constitutes our goals, what you want to accomplish to give meaning and achievement to our mission. Goals are usually long range, perhaps reaching as much as several years into the future. But, foggy as they may seem in the distance, you need them to help determine what intermediate steps you're going to take . . . and why.

Goals are usually described in general terms; for example, "develop a stronger domestic customer base." Whenever possible, you should quantify these goals. What does a "stronger customer base" mean? What is it now? How much larger do you want it to be? Is that realistic?

With each of your goals set, again ask the vital question: "why." If the goals don't fit in with the accomplishment of your mission, you either have to change your mission or change your goals. Your mission and goals must be compatible, or you're starting to float again.

As these judgments are made, it's valuable to include several members of the organization in the planning process. How many people will be involved will depend on the size of the organization, but your concern should be to encourage participation from those who will be responsible for carrying out the mission once it is determined.

People tend to give more support—more commitment—to something they help create. It's wise to include not only senior management people, but middle managers, supervisors, and even non-managerial employees in the planning process. Lower echelon employees often can offer significant input from an often overlooked perspective. They're closer to the action and see aspects that people higher up may miss.

Your goals will give you something to focus on. They will provide strategic direction to your organization so you can see where you're headed on a long-range basis. Your goals will give meaning to your mission. Their accomplishment gives life and vitality to you and your organization.

Moving toward Results

Your next step is to divide your goals into more manageable portions. Now you'll be setting objectives which, as accomplished, will move you closer to the achievement of your goals. Objectives are the steps along the path to goal fulfillment.

At this stage, you should add the quantitative elements to your plan. By incorporating task measurements and schedules, you make your plan more legitimate. Having clearer definitions will make it easier to gain acceptance of your plan, especially if you have involved a cross-section of your people in the planning process. Check yourself: do you know specifically what results you desire, how well you wish to achieve them, and how to tell when your objectives are met?

Here again, you should ask "why," to be sure you're staying on target. Apply the "why" test to your schedules, as well. Why do you want to accomplish certain objectives by certain dates? If you try to move too quickly in one area, you may invest a disproportionate amount of your resources in reaching a lower priority objective.

Your objectives, as your goals, should be prioritized. In fact, everything you do should be prioritized, at least in your mind. You may find it helpful to put your priorities down on paper so you can see what's most important for you to do. This is discussed further in the chapter on Priority and Time Management.

As you begin to look at implementation of your plan, you will be allocating resources to the accomplishment of your objectives. You have to understand your priorities, timetable, and actual resource needs to properly move forward. Be sure you can see how the whole plan fits together and how the pieces relate to each other.

Let me share a couple of metaphors that will illustrate the goals/objectives/action steps design. If we bake a wonderful cherry pie, our task is to eat it. It is impossible to put the entire pie into our mouth at one time—there's just too much. So, we cut it into slices so we can better manage the consumption process. Alas, the portions are still too large to take in all at once. Finally we cut the slices into bite-sized pieces. Now we can begin to eat our delicious pie. Ice cream, anyone?

In this illustration, the pie represents the goal, the slice represents the objective, and the bite represents the action step. As we eat the bites, we eat the slices, and eventually we consume the entire scrumptious pie. As we complete the action steps, we accomplish our objectives, and eventually achieve the goals.

In my seminars I also put the three levels of planning tools into a time-oriented perspective. The goals are the strategies. The top of the mountain is our strategic level; we're high enough that we can see great distances into the future, while we can be highly aware of our past and present. Strategic management must work from this position, carefully using the respected ability to see far into the distance—ahead, behind, and parallel.

The objectives are tactics, utilized by tactical managers found about half-way up the mountain. These managers see enough to interpret what the managers see, but can also allocate resources that will be needed by people occupying the levels beneath them. In the foothills are the action steps, carried out by workers on the front line.

In this metaphorical presentation, I explain that strategic managers think, plan, and act based on their long-range view. Their perspective is typically three to five years into the future. Tactical managers focus on a time period ranging from a couple of months out to up to three years. This is a medium-range view that focuses on a component of the strategic view. The operational or front-line managers concentrate on the immediate, up to a short-range concern of perhaps a couple of months.

Focusing on Tasks

Next, we look at what actually has to be done to accomplish our objectives. These step-by-step tasks are the action steps that will go hand-in-hand with your expectations of each employee.

Each employee should have a say in the design of his/her expectations. Not only will this personal involvement assure that the employee can fulfill the expectation, but a sense of commitment is developed as each person agrees that he/she can and will accomplish the task(s) assigned and accepted. You are building a sense of ownership among your people that they will meet their responsibilities. They have a personal stake, since they helped determine those expected results.

The individual efforts of each employee are expressed in the specific tasks. The work should be measurable and easily understood by all concerned. Everyone, especially the front- line employee, should be comfortable that the tasks can be accomplished as expected. Be sure you are gaining commitment, lip service.

Each of the tasks should be carefully related to the accomplishment of a mutually understood objective. People need to appreciate how their efforts contribute to the whole. Enable them to see the importance of their task(s) and your chances of achieving your results will be practically guaranteed.

A word of warning is appropriate here. Beware of those employees who just go along with what you are saying because it seems the proper—or least difficult—thing to do. Explain that you are entering into an agreement with them that they have the competence, capacity, and desire to complete the specified tasks in the time allotted. You, and many others are counting on them. Invest whatever time is necessary to confirm your mutual understanding.

So, the process is to establish a four-tiered plan. The foundation tier, if you will, is the mission and vision. Everything else flows from this core. Everything else must be consistent with and supportive of the mission and vision.

Goals are far-reaching: our long-term strategy. Goals are accomplished by the achievement of objectives. Objectives are met through completion of action steps. I compare the concept to a cherry pie. (I like cherry pie, especially warm . . . with ice cream!) Our goal is to eat the entire pie. We can't put the whole thing in our mouth, so we'll cut it into slices (objectives). That's still a pretty big portion; we can't possibly take it all in at once. So, we cut the slices into bite-size pieces. These pieces represent our action steps. So how do you eat that scrumptious cherry pie? One bite at a time. How do you handle big projects? One action step at a time.

This approach to project management, to company management, to life management, is wonderfully interchangeable. You can apply the same process to practically anything you do. Planning a vacation trip? Mapping out the emergence of a new company? Picking out the clothes you'll wear tomorrow? The same system applies to all these cases and, of course, many more.

In the corporate setting, we're seeing increased concern about management, particularly as we struggle to look into the future and manage well in the short-term. Is management legitimate? authentic? Is management "connected" with the non-management people who work for the company? Are they "singing from the same sheet of music?" If the people working for an organization are congruent in their thinking, their values, their attitudes, their approach, their goals, there is a much stronger potential for high achievement and high satisfaction.

The secret to achieving this congruence, this consistency, is for senior leaders to share their philosophies with the people who work with them. Too often we assume that everybody knows who we are and where we're going. Wrong! The reality is quite different. Frankly, most employees today have little or no idea where the company is going or how it hopes to get there.

What's wrong with this picture? Management is bounding along the path it set for itself, assuming that everyone else is following dutifully right behind them. Sorry, it doesn't work that way; people don't follow anyone unquestionably today. There is precious little blind acceptance to the idea that whatever management says must be right.

Today's employees, particularly young people, will challenge the status quo. They'll ask, almost belligerently, for an explanation of what your company is all about . . . and how they are expected to fit into this paradigm. They'll ask, "What's in it for me, in ways that challenge your thinking, your planning, your very approach to doing business. How prepared are you to articulate what your company is all about. what that means to you, and what it means to the various people working with you.

Thinking about what you just read, your inclination may be to spend some time in your back office to put something down in your statements of what you want to do. That's counterproductive, since you want to collaborate with your employees to create a missions statement that more fully represents how you all feel about your company.

Thought-Provoking Questions

1. Why must a clear sense of direction be defined and understood before people can help an organization excel?
2. Define the underlying philosophies and principles of your organization. How can you share these beliefs with your people?
3. How can you relate daily activities to long term goals and objectives?
4. For more ideas about what you can do with your company's mission statement, contact the author, Roger E. Herman, at his e-mail address: roger@herman.net, or phone 1-800-227-3566. Please identify yourself so Roger can call you to ask questions. Thank you.

Reader's Notes

6

Clarity of Expectations

With your goals, objectives, and action steps established, it's now time to clarify your expectations of each member of your team. This clarification is a vital part of creating the environment most conducive to excelling. People want to know exactly what is expected of them in the workplace so they can do what they're supposed to do.

To strengthen your position, enable each member of your team to understand what is expected of the team as a whole, of other teams, and of the collection of all the teams—the organization. Help them see why they're doing what they're doing, how it relates to what others are doing, and how it connects to produce an end product or service. Remember, your people want to know how they fit into the "big picture" of what your organization is doing.

Your expectations of each employee will, of course, be

based on the fulfillment of the action steps, objectives, goals, and mission statement. Each employee should be familiar with the organization's overall mission and plan. They'll be better team members if they can see that they are playing an important role, that they're an integral part of the overall system.

An effective way to help employees comprehend the "big picture" is to give them an all-encompassing tour of your company. Explain how the company gets business, how the orders come in, and how they're processed for invoicing and manufacturing (or service). Tell them about the purchasing function and show them how materials are brought in at the receiving area. After they get a look at how materials move into processing or are moved into another area for stocking, show employees each step of the process. Show them all the important areas of the company, including accounting, customer service, maintenance, and the president's office. Define what happens in each place so learners can put the pieces together in their minds. Message: it's valuable to help blue color workers appreciate that white collar and pink collar workers do real work, and vice-versa.

The tour for new employees should include the manufacturing (or service areas so people can see how products are produced and services are provided. If a part of the company's work is done off-site—in retail stores, warehouses or on routes, for example it would be valuable for employees to understand what happens in these remote areas. After they've seen the whole picture, introduce them to their work responsibilities. Help them relate their particular job to the mission of the company. As they comprehend the importance of their role, they will be more dedicated to performing as an integral part of the corporate team.

Obviously, the elements of what you do will be different for each company, but you get the picture. Help your new people understand how the whole system works, then show them what their role is. This approach enables each worker to appreciate the value and importance of the work they do—as it interconnects with everything else the company does. This knowledge substantially reduces the "it's just another job" attitude and raises self-esteem as people recognize that others are depending on them to do their part. Absenteeism drops when workers know others are relying on them so the whole company can function.

When people see that "big picture," it's also easier for them to spot ways to improve the way your company does business. Educated employees—educated in what you're trying to do in your business—can offer valuable suggestions for doing things better, differently, or for different reasons. They'll have a better view of company functions now, as well as thinking and planning toward future success.

This process will enhance the work relationship for your new employees. How about your current employees? In almost every company I've served as a management consultant, I've discovered long-term employees who had never been out of their departments. These valued employees had no idea what else went on in the company. They just did their own job, without feeling a part of anything larger than their own work unit.

Clarify through Shared Planning

Expectations can be clarified during the company's planning process. Most organizations plan their work on at least an annual basis. Many revisit their plan more frequently, just to be sure they're on target. Conscious planning should be accomplished on a periodic basis as part of the cycle of the way the company functions—it's just good business practice. Share with each employee what the company is striving to do.

Relate this orientation of current work and future plans to what the employee is doing personally as part of the company's operation. Invite each team member to design and commit to what he/she will do to help achieve the desired results.

Through this process the employee actually has a say in what work will be done and how it will be measured. This involvement will be powerful when performance appraisal time rolls around—you'll evaluate workers on how well they accomplished what they said they would do.

Employee input into the planning process can be done on an individual or on a group basis, depending on the type of organization, tasks to be accomplished, interrelationships, and other circumstances that may be unique to your situation. Your objective should be to reach an agreement with each employee regarding expectations.

Include what you and your team member should expect of each other to assure that both of you, and others with whom you relate, are working at peak performance.

Avoid making the experience a one-way communication, with you telling your subordinates what they're going to do. Don't keep them in the dark until it's time to start work. ["Mushroom Management" is the term used to describe how we manage people like we grow mushrooms: keep them in the dark and throw plenty of manure on them.] Provide opportunities for your people to openly and constructively express their feelings about how they see the job to be done.

Be receptive to alternative approaches proposed by your people. They are closer to the "action" and will have a better idea of what can be done, how quickly it can be done, and how it can be done most efficiently and effectively. Focus your expectations more on results than on the specifics of how the job gets done. Try to give your workers some flexibility to design their own work, seeking your support as necessary to achieve their objectives.

For years, managers have been trained to give people answers. The more effective approach, we've learned, is to give them support instead. Clarify what's expected, give them what they need to perform, then get out of their way! See chapter 10 for further discussion of this approach.

In your discussions with your subordinates, constantly

seek to reduce ambiguity and uncertainty of what is to be done. Talk about what you expect of your people and encourage your people to express what they expect of you as their manager. Move past the kinds of things that are addressed in the typical job description. Open conversations about attitude, collaboration, creativity, and problem-solving. Stimulate thinking about how each of your people can really become an even more effective member of the team.

You need to engage in similar discussions with your superior. If you are not clear about what is expected of you, you will have difficulty communicating expectations clearly to your subordinates. Remember, your subordinates are really extensions of you in getting your organization's work done. Your boss may be uncomfortable with this process—at least at first. You may need to explain how clarifying expectations works. Maybe you should give your boss a copy of this book to read!

Many people who are in "boss" positions have risen through the ranks over the years to attain their current job. They've been carefully taught to direct and demand. Engaging in conversations about what people expect of each other, about relationships, about what the company is striving to accomplish, are foreign to the more traditional style of management. Don't be discouraged if you don't get the full response you desire in your first meeting with your boss. Habits build up over a long period of time; they change almost as slowly.

Unclear expectations are like an out-of-focus picture on a television set. You've got a general idea of what's going on, but you're not really sure about it. You can't see the details, the fine points, that make a significant difference. Take the initiative to be sure expectations are in focus for everyone with whom you work. "Everyone" means people in other departments with whom you interact. It could also mean suppliers and customers.

When all stakeholders understand the big picture, work

becomes more like a smooth flow instead of a sputter.

Understand that at first your subordinates may be reluctant to discuss some of these matters with you. They may have fears of showing incompetence or a too-limited understanding of their job, team, or organization. Many workers have been taught or "socialized" not to talk with the boss about company matters. "Just keep your nose clean, do what you're told, and everything will be fine."

You might have to work patiently with some of your people over a period of time before they'll open up and seriously discuss the components of their job with you. Let them know that it's now appropriate for the two of you to agree on what the job expectations should be . . . and that you welcome employee input. Emphasize the nature of your collaborative partnership.

Once you have determined—with the employee—what is expected, don't make changes unilaterally. If changes seem to be needed, evaluate the situation with the employee in an open, two-way discussion. Listen carefully to your employee's point of view. Make any needed changes together, so there is clear expectation and commitment from everyone involved.

The person responsible for getting a job done should logically have the greatest say in how it will be accomplished. If the end results will meet your needs, give the employee the freedom to proceed independently. You may discover that your subordinates have a lot more insight and talent than you've been giving them credit for having.

In a medium-sized manufacturing firm I served as a consultant, a key employee was frustrated because the president wouldn't listen to his ideas or give him more freedom to determine how he could do his job. Not knowing just what the boss really wanted from him, he pulled back, taking less and less initiative. The boss moved in to fill the vacuum, never bothering to ask for the employee's input or participation. The unenlightened company president did the same thing with other key employees. It wasn't long before the president had assumed an overwhelming load of responsibility—and work. Key employees began to describe themselves as mediocre because they really couldn't do much of what they had felt were their jobs in the company. A gradual erosion of spirit and performance among the key people dampened the effectiveness of the company.

Years later, with the company in serious trouble, the key employees finally persuaded the president to relinquish some of what he had been doing. He was reluctant to do so at first, feeling that others could not do the job as well as he could. To his amazement, his people fulfilled the responsibilities even better than he had been doing them! With a greatly reduced workload and re-energized employees, the president was able to cut back to a more reasonable work week. Efficiency and effectiveness returned; customer satisfaction, sales, *and* profits increased dramatically.

As a management consultant, I've seen this scenario many times. I've observed it in all kinds of companies, large and small. Sometimes owners and senior executives unwittingly get in their own way! My advice: hire well, clarify expectations, train and equip people to do their jobs, then trust them to perform. If they don't perform, take whatever action is necessary. But, that action does *not* include doing their jobs for them. Either they do their jobs, or their replacements do. You do not. You have your own job to do.

When people have a clear understanding of what's expected of them, and the support they need from their superiors, they'll usually do an outstanding job. Look closely at the most successful companies you know and you'll discover that people see the big picture, they know what's expected of them, and they have an agreement about what they can expect from others. The results are tremendous!

You can experience this kind of success story in your organization by letting your employees exercise some initiative and ingenuity in how they do their jobs. Your concern as a manager should be focused on the end results, not on the details of how the work is performed. Once you and your subordinates agree on what should be done, get out of the way and let them perform. As your people do their jobs, without your needing to hold their hands, you will have more confidence and time to do your job.

Some organizations have found great success in developing, cooperatively with the employee, written performance plans. These plans specify what the employee will accomplish within a given period of time. Included are routine responsibilities, projects to be worked on and/or completed, and a timetable for completion.

In some cases, the employee's personal development plan is also included in the corporate performance plan. This acknowledgment confirms that continued learning and growth is part of the employee's responsibility. The foundation of the document can be the employee's job description; current activities can be shown as applications of the standardized set of job expectations.

Be sure at the start of any project, and at any other time it seems necessary, that you clarify with your employees exactly what you expect. Take the extra time to personally sit down with people and deliberately share expectations. With the fast pace today, it may seem unnecessarily burdensome to stop and invest that extra individual time.

If you pause, physically, to communicate with your team members, you'll discover that they'll do a better job for you. Explain what you want done—how quickly, to what level of quality, at what price, etc.? When people understand the criteria for measuring their performance, they'll respond.

People function much more productively in an environment where expectations are clear. They are be more consciously involved in an environment where they have realistic input into how their job will be done. People work more closely together when there is a feeling of meaningful involvement on the part of the entire work group.

If you want people to excel, give them the freedom to suggest how to make the best use of their knowledge, skills, and abilities on the job. Let them know you want the best they have to offer: that's one of your expectations. Ask what they need from you to enable them to excel. Their response will tell you some of the expectations they have of you.

When mutual expectations are clarified and met for people who work together, individuals, teams, and organizations excel.

Thought-Provoking Questions

1. When should you clarify for your people what you except from them? Why?
2. What do others expect from you? How can you confirm agreement on mutual expectations? What value would such an agreement hold?
3. How much should expectations be reduced to writing? Why? Consider both positives and negative aspects of this process, both long-term and short-term.

Reader's Notes

7

Results-Oriented Leadership

Now that you have a clear sense of your organization's mission, and your goals and objectives are set, you can focus your energy on achieving results. Setting and reaching mission-supporting goals and objectives is a powerful aspect of excelling as a manager, as a leader. Autocratic and charismatic leaders may have high profiles and get a lot of attention, but the true measure is how well you get the job done.

Whether you are an individual, a manager, an executive, a business owner or play any other role in life, you want to see some sort of return on investment of your time, energy, and knowledge. This drive, this desire, this sense of accomplishment dates 'way back to our ancestors' ancestors. Even the cave dwellers, when they went forth on their hunting and gathering expeditions, wanted to come back with something to show for their efforts.

Through the generations, this desire for recognizable achievement has persisted. We all possess it in one form or another. Getting things done is a critical measure of our effectiveness as human beings. It's part of our self-esteem. We all want to achieve results, but sometimes we don't know what results are appropriate. This uncertainty is particularly prevalent in organizational settings, where leaders fail to share enough information with their people to get those people focused.

Applying results-oriented leadership, all of your energies and resources are directed toward the accomplishment of expectations. Included are expectations others have of us, as well as our own personal standards of performance. Our personal activities should be designed to help us achieve our specific goals and objectives, whether those desired results are based in our work, organization, family, community, or some other context. In the corporate arena, everything we do must serve to strengthen our work group's forward movement toward clear objectives.

If you have an opportunity (or a temptation) to do something that doesn't move you toward attaining your results, seriously challenge and question investing your time and energy in that activity. Justify everything you do as legitimate effort moving toward the specific end results for which you are responsible.

Too many managers—and non-managers—allow themselves to be led astray from what they really should be doing. As a result, their efforts are diluted; they do not perform as well as they could as leaders. They don't feel a strong sense of purpose and control in their work lives; and, understandably, they do not transmit a sense of targeted commitment to their people. Without this concentration on results, it's easy to understand why so many organizations, guided by such unfocused people, drift or flounder.

Determining and Sharing Targets

An expression attributed to a number of glib folks is "If you don't know where you're going, any path will take you there." That is so true! Shared determination of desired results, and the paths to achieve them, are so powerful. As I often quote in my consulting work, "People support what they help to create." In *The Process of Excelling*, Element 1 (A Sense of Direction) and Element 7 (Involvement) are vitally important to the redesigning of where you're going and how you're going to get there. Then, of course, Element 2 (Clarity of Expectations) bubbles to the surface. Yes, all the elements of the process are complicatedly interconnected.

More and more companies are discovering great success from sharing heretofore private information with the people who work for them. This practice is know as "open book management." Some employers share everything with their people; others are more selective about what is shared, for a variety of reasons. A caution here is that whatever is shared must also be explained—explained so it can be understood as part of the "big picture," in a way that the specifics of the data make sense.

Avoid the temptation to share everything at once. Spewing out confusing data to everyone will be overwhelming, irritating, and counterproductive. Introduce your sharing process gradually, giving people time to comprehend and relate each piece of information. Concentrate on those aspects that have meaning for those who will gain the knowledge and insight. Invest. Take whatever time is necessary to assure that people understand what you're sharing, what it means, and how it relates to their work and their future. Show them how to use the information to better measure and improve the company's performance.

When consulting with my corporate clients about sharing numbers, I recommend that emphasis be placed on key results areas. The question I ask is "How do we know if we're doing a good job?" What do we measure that tells us how well we're doing? Let's share that information with everyone who might be able to influence our results. if there are preliminary measures that contribute to our principal measurements, let's track those and share that data, too.

Once people understand data they can relate to—and do something with, they will be more receptive and appreciative of what you share with them. The sharing experience has to have meaning for everyone, or it's a waste of time. Don't fall into the trap of eagerly sharing knowledge that no one else really wants. That shoving of data into people's faces will turn them off, and may even turn them against you.

"MBDA"

The solution to this problem is delightfully simple: know what you're trying to accomplish, why you're doing it, how you're going to get it done, and when you're expected to show results. Once people have the information they need regarding what we're about, the challenge is to laser-focus everyone's energies on getting the job done. Then, manage by deliberate action (MBDA). Let's look at the components of "Management by Deliberate Action."

The first word of the technique of MBDA is "management". The classic definition of management is "getting things done through other people". But it's more than that. You're also responsible for planning, organizing, and applying other resources such as space, equipment, raw materials, time, and energy. Management includes monitoring the production of your work group, coordinating adjustments as needed to consistently produce desired results.

Management also suggests having a different perspective of the organization and of your job. It's a special kind of responsibility. In your management role, you're not really supposed to "work" anymore. There's a significant change in role from performing principal tasks to orchestrating the work of a number of people. Your job is to help other people, who are, in turn, accountable to you, to get their work done. You collaborate with other leaders—your peers and your superiors—is to coordinate your work group's activities with those of other work groups in, and sometimes outside of your organization.

There are many different ways to manage people and other resources. Textbooks are filled with theories . . . and insight into the practical application of those theories. Dedicated managers who really want to excel in their fields invest their time to read books, magazines, and newsletters about management and leadership. They attend seminars and courses to improve their understanding and their skills.

Build your own competencies and learn about the various management styles to determine what is best for you. Consider which style(s) would be most comfortable and most effective for you and your work environment. Become conversant in current thinking in the field of management; there are a variety of changes and trends that bear watching. Most proponents of good management today prefer team leadership and people-oriented styles over outmoded autocratic approaches. People want to hear their managers support them, not confront them with messages akin to "my way or the highway."

Deliberate

The next important word of the MBDA technique is "deliberate". Everything you do should be deliberate and purposeful. Focus your efforts on achieving specific accomplishments. Do what you do intentionally, with a clear understanding of why you are doing it and how it fits in with other things you are doing.

An amazing number of managers do things "by accident", rather than deliberately. They are reactive in their style, rather than being proactive. Things just happen, without much carefully planned leadership from the manager. Sometimes those things are productive; sometimes they're not. If results are achieved by the work group, the achievement may be in spite of your efforts rather than because of what you do. The team doesn't reach its full capacity. Workers sense the lack of deliberate leadership and their damped motivation is reflected in their lower performance.

When you perform deliberately, you know exactly where you and your work group are going. You have planned the use of your resources with sufficient knowledge and detail to assure that few things, if any, "fall through the cracks." The efforts of the work group are focused, organized and scheduled so maximum productivity is achieved.

Subordinates feel good about working for a deliberate manager. You demonstrate that you know what you are doing. Rarely must inadequate work be redone, few resources are wasted, and your people feel a sense of purpose about what they're doing. This deliberate action builds people's confidence—and enthusiasm—in following you as their leader. They are happy to know that things happen on purpose, rather than by accident.

Action

The last word of MBDA is "action." Excelling management is action-oriented. As an action-oriented manager, you work on the front lines with your people and support them to achieve the team's objectives. You take action when it's appropriate, rather than procrastinating and hoping the problems will just go away.

Managers who aren't action-oriented have little or no influence over their work groups. They simply sit back and let people "do their thing." They concentrate on keeping records and doing other paperwork, managing their area of responsibility from behind their desks. They aren't in touch with what's happening in their work group or in the organization. They react to problems, rather than plan ahead to avoid them (we call this behavior "management by crisis"— it's more prevalent than you'd imagine). Their subordinates don't really know them, and there may be alienation or an adversarial relationship between the manager and his/her people. Without action, these managers are not really involved. They're just there.

Management of a work group is a dynamic experience. Things are always changing, shifting this way or that. Sometimes it's a raw materials concern; in other situations it may be a people problem, financial concerns, scheduling issues, or any one of a number of other challenges that confront an assertive high-achieving work group.

Recognizing that problems won't simply evaporate, excelling managers gather the information they need, make a decision, then act upon that decision. Action comes rather quickly, but they can't wait until things get out of hand. They must respond rapidly when a prompt response is needed.

If you are an excelling manager, you are fortunate: people respect and appreciate your action-oriented style. They like knowing that you are "in touch" and won't let things get out of hand.

Taking quick action doesn't mean shooting from the hip. Remember that MBDA includes deliberation. The actions taken are very deliberate, carefully thought-out as well as direct. Whenever necessary, you do take action. When something has to be done, you don't hide or turn to mush. You actively take responsibility and control to assure results. Your employees will have confidence in you as you practice the MBDA concept, because they know you are certain where you are going, and they are comfortable following you.

Leadership versus Managership

Managers may do a fine job coordinating all their resources, following schedules to meet deadlines, and have all the details well in hand. They have things under control, and may even be admired for their efficiency. However, they may not be leaders.

Leadership involves working closely with people. It means people follow you because they want to, because they have confidence in you. They believe you know what you're doing and have dedicated yourself to helping them achieve their goals. They respect your knowledge and are proud of you and the way you operate.

People working for leaders feel more a part of what's happening, because their leaders keep them informed. The sharing of information and ideas is a two-way street, benefiting all concerned. Employees feel a part of what's happening. They experience a special sense of belonging that motivates them to be more dedicated to excelling in the work they do for you and for your organization.

Leaders are sensitive, staying alert for signals about how things are going in the work group. When problems arise, leaders respond assertively to solve the problems before they become serious. Listen to your people to gain a full understanding of situations before taking action. Observing this sensitivity, your people will feel comfortable about communicating necessary information to you, without fear of consequences.

As a results-oriented leader, strive for consistency and cooperation. Appreciate that many of your people need stability and support; work consciously to fulfill those needs. Don't make frequent changes that are unsettling to your subordinates. Your people should be able to rely on you to act in an intelligent, mature manner to help them achieve the desired results.

Organizations that are led by teams of results-oriented leaders have a special kind of corporate spirit. It's not a pep rally kind of spirit. Rather, it's a sort of focus and devotion to getting the right things done, the right way, on time . . . because it's the thing to do. That kind of spirit builds a pride in achievement—high achievement—that serves as a source of continual motivation and strength. That deep sense of laser-like energy is unconquerably powerful.

The more managers in an organization who adopt the principles of results-oriented leadership and MBDA, the stronger the organization will be. The synergy creates a force of multiple energies, rather than merely the sum of the committed leaders.

A Vital Result: Good Customer Service

While quite a bit has been said and written about customer service, this important focus deserves mention in this chapter. Customer service can be a unifying force to build the level of organizational congruence that will be the envy of your competitors.

Make service to your customers—internal and external—your primary objective. Providing outstanding service to both is essential. Delighting your customers is a critical component of short-term and long-term success. Without your customers, there is no reason for your organization to exist. And without the existence of your organization, there would be no jobs for you or your people.

Identifying external customers is easy. They are the individuals and/or companies who purchase the product or service that your organization produces for consumption in the marketplace. These are the people who pay the bills, so they must be satisfied whenever and however possible. If you don't satisfy them, your competitors will certainly go after their business.

There is a fallacy in the thinking of many people working in our organizations today. They seem to think that satisfying the customer is the job of the salespeople or management. While those key players have their role, it has become increasingly apparent that everyone in your organization shares a part of that responsibility. Customer service is everybody's business! Everyone in your organization serves the external customer or serves those who do serve the external customer.

Internal customers are those people and departments you serve within your own organization. While they may not pay your bills the same way as external customers, they deserve the same consideration from you. Today's organizations are so interdependent that all elements must function well together if the entity is to succeed.

You and your team members may be well advised to visit your customers, both internal and external. Develop personal relationships. Learn how your product or service is used by your customer(s). You may be able to offer some suggestions that will make your work or theirs more efficient or effective. In every way that you can, demonstrate that you care on a level of personal accountability.

Part of your job as an excelling leader is to always be sensitive to your various customers, and assure that all your team members share your sensitivity and concern. Even little things like the way the telephone is answered can make a difference in a customer's perception of you. A high level of professionalism is desired, but less than the best is expected as a fact of life. Deliver at a high standard and you'll easily gain positive attention!

Seek ways that you and your team can demonstrate extra care for your customers. Strive to do things right the first time. Pay attention to all those little details. Expect the customer to be picky; take steps to assure that there is little or nothing with which to find fault in your results.

A parting thought on customer service: "The customer may not always be right, but he's never wrong."

Thought-Provoking Questions

1. How well is MBDA used in your organization? What results do you perceive?
2. What is the difference between managing and leading?
3. How can you sharpen your focus on desired results?

Reader's Notes

8

Initiative,
Responsibility,
and Accountability

Today people want more control in their lives. They want to feel responsible for significant aspects of their employment, of their home lives, and of their personal lives. As a leader, you can improve your employees' sense of self-worth by giving them more responsibility.

Along with that responsibility must go the authority to fulfill the agreed-upon expectations. When given the appropriate authority, your people will know that they really are expected to respond. They'll see that the assignment of responsibility is not just "lip service," but as legitimate, clear, and empowering.

Don't feel threatened by your subordinates having authority. You will grow as they do. The better they perform, the better you'll look. Their power to perform tasks still flows from you; you're still in charge. And you're still ultimately responsible. Delegation of power and authority is not abdication; it's sharing.

The other key factor in this formula is personal accountability. It's important that people at all levels of the organization understand this vital concept. There will be those who will be delighted to have some important responsibility, but won't want to be held accountable for their actions. That's an unacceptable arrangement. Those who desire responsibility *must* accept accountability as well. Those two functions go together unequivocally.

Where to Start

The best approach is to begin with a level of responsibility that is manageable for both you and your subordinate. Then, as the employee proves capable, more responsibility, authority, and accountability can be assigned. It's a gradual process. Sometimes the growth comes quickly; sometimes it takes a while. Work with each individual to develop him/her as fast as the employee is able to grow.

What the employee becomes responsible for, over time, will depend on the organization's needs, your confidence in the employee's ability to handle more responsibility, and the employee's interest. Seek assignments that will be reasonable for your people, but challenging as well. That will aid personal and professional growth and build confidence. Even if the employee is a little bit afraid of the new responsibility, you will be giving strength by showing your confidence that the job can be done. Your attitude will be picked-up by the worker who, in turn, will become more confident.

Whenever you assign a responsibility, take extra care to be very clear in your expectations. Explain, in whatever detail may be appropriate, what is to be done and why, when it should be done, and to whom the employee is accountable for the assignment's results. Share your ideas about how you feel the job should be done (unless you're leaving that determination to the discretion of the employee).

Don't simply assign the responsibility, then not support the employee. Provide the clear authority to perform the task and assure that all needed resources are available. As the assigning manager, you have a personal obligation to serve as coach as your team member moves forward to accomplish the task. Encourage your employee, provide counsel as needed, and accept the reality (with the employee) that failure or less than total success is a possibility.

Risk versus Failure

Many people mistakenly believe that failure or inadequate achievement is forbidden in work organizations. As a result, they are afraid to take initiatives, accept responsibilities, or be held accountable. While you certainly don't want to encourage failure, it is vital that you communicate a permission to risk failure or initiative will be dampened.

You can quote expressions such as "no pain, no gain" and "no guts, no glory" all day long. But, until your people believe that you mean it, they won't stick their necks out. One way to explain your encouragement of innovation and risk taking is to describe the turtle: As long as he's safe in his shell, all tucked in and closed up, the turtle won't be able to go anywhere. In order to move from where he is, the turtle must stick his neck out.

Within limits, which you can describe to your people, encourage them to stick their necks out. Try new ways of doing things, be alert to new ideas and approaches, design and test new systems. As you observe others taking initiative, even if it's just to do something relatively routine without being asked, praise that initiative. As Michael LeBoeuf tells us in his book, ***The Greatest Management Principle in*** *the World*, people will do what they are encouraged to do by their supervisor's reinforcement of desired actions.

Here's an idea. Get some posters of turtles, stuffed turtles, plastic or ceramic turtles. Put them in your office and display them in other areas of the building. Send them to people in the field. Use the turtle as a sort of icon to remind people to stick their necks out . . . that they're protected by their hard shells. Make it a positive expression.

Remember that a key to inspiring creativity and initiative among your people is to be receptive to their new ideas. Nourish their thinking and bolster their performance in whatever ways seem appropriate. Your goal is to send a clear message that you respect the insight and mental capacity of your people and want to see those strengths used to improve working conditions and productivity.

Some people need practice and experience in thinking about specific challenges, considering alternative approaches, and following through with action to achieve results. For various reasons, many workers in organizations never perceive that they have such an opportunity. They don't believe they're allowed to indulge in such practices; they've gotten the message over the years that they should simply do what they're told to do. You, as their leader, can deliberately create exciting opportunities for them to try new things and achieve inspiring successes.

The method we use to create opportunities for people to grow, to take initiative, is called delegation. Done well, the delegation process will get them started, to make them comfortable with creative thought, responsibility, and follow-through. Effective delegation involves carefully following a purposeful procedure. Consider the various aspects of delegation carefully; it's not as easy as most managers think it is (which is why many managers are not effective delegators).

The Formula for Success

As I've consulted with various companies, I've discovered an interesting dichotomy.

Leaders want their people to take initiative, yet they don't delegate effectively. The two concepts of initiative and delegation are intertwined. Consider this equation:

$$I = R + A + A$$

Initiative = Responsibility + Authority + Accountability. *All three* elements must be present to generate initiative. The responsibilty must be clear and concise. The authority, the power to get things done, must be accepted by the protegé. The person accepting the delegation must make that decision to be accountable consciously and overtly to the delegator. When all these elements are present, you will have delegation. If they are not all legitimately present, you will not have delegation.

How to Delegate

When delegating work to other people, it is important to follow a series of steps to do the job effectively. There are a number of elements of the delegation experience you should be sure to include in your relationship with your delegate. Here are the procedures to follow:

1. Determine Objectives

Know what you want to accomplish—concrete results that you can describe to someone else. Know also *why* you want to delegate this particular task: to reduce your work load, to groom a subordinate, to familiarize others with the task, to get others involved, or perhaps because someone else can do it better than you can.

2. Select Delegate

Decide to whom you want to delegate the selected objective or task. Think about how that person will react when you actually make the delegation assignment. Prepare to respond to anticipated concerns, building comfort with the assignment.

In some cases, you may have to "sell" the idea to your subordinate. Having been burned too many times during their careers, many employees resist accepting delegation. Build in the *want-to*; get the horse thirsty before you lead it to water and the horse will drink much better.

3. Assign Duties and Grant Appropriate Authority

Present the task in results-oriented terms. Explain the end results you desire, not how to get the job done. The "how" is up to the delegate. Be clear about what you expect and when you expect the work to be completed. Assign sufficient authority and provide sufficient access to information to enable your delegate to get the job done.

When assigning authority, clarify what that authority is and how to use it. Be sure that others with whom your delegate will interact also know that you have granted the authority to get a job done. It is frustrating and demeaning for an employee to have to come back to you for support in convincing others that the authority really has been granted. Avoid putting your delegate in that embarrassing position.

4. Educate Your Delegate and Establish Necessary Controls

Give your delegate as much information and insight as you can to make it easier for the job to be done. Encourage the delegate to give some thought to how the task will be approached, then get together to discuss it. Support the delegate's strategy, even if you don't agree with it. The important thing is that the delegate is gaining some invaluable experience in examining desired goals, considering alternative methodologies for accomplishing the goals, and actually planning work ahead of time for greater results.

If you're not comfortable with the proposed planned approach, ask questions to stimulate the delegate to think more about what will be done. *Don't just give delegates your solutions to their problems; insist people think things through for themselves.* That's how they grow, building the confidence to take initiative on their own.

Be prepared, psychologically, to deal with uncertainty, hesitancy, reluctance. and even conscious resistance. Don't tell your subordinate the "right" way to think, plan, implement, or behave. Help your people discern this valuable perspective for themselves by asking questions, offering empathy and encouragement, and stepping back out of the way.

5. Monitor and Adjust

Schedule regular meetings for the delegate to give you progress reports and seek your advice and counsel. Be available in the interim if the delegate needs your support. Remember that the delegate is an extension of you; the ultimate responsibility still belongs to you. You cannot abdicate that responsibility.

If the delegate is off-track, question and guide rather than direct. If you're going to get personally involved by giving specific directions, you might as well do the job yourself.

Avoid the "NIH"—not-invented-here syndrome. Accept the fact that others, including perhaps people you've just hired, may have a different style or approach than you do. Respect their perspectives and allow that there may be many paths to the same desired end result.

6. Evaluate/Praise

Upon completion of the assignment, praise the delegate for the job that was done. Celebrate your (collective) achievements. Bask in the warmth of completion. Revel in the process and the results achieved, and quickly move on to delegate another responsibility to reinforce the worker's capacity to serve as a viable member of the team.

The more difficult role for you as a leader is to address those who have not become efffective in delegating or in accepting delegation. Let's explore some concerns and techniques to deal with less than satisfactory performance.

Even if it wasn't perfect, still deliver the praise! Compliment the delegate on being willing to undertake the assignment, on the process that was followed correctly, and on what was done well. If you focus on positive aspects, your delegate will be motivated to try other new challenges, even if success wasn't complete in this opportunity.

In those cases where a delegate falls short of your expectations, you still need to provide support. Avoid chastising. Instead, strive to help the employee feel good about what *was* accomplished and seek ways to perform better in the future. Feelings can be fragile, so demonstrate your caring and support to help them accept their shortcomings. Immediately begin to strengthen the employee's capacity to accept a similar challenge in the future.

A valuable technique to apply, particularly when an employee has fallen short of an intended objective, is to immediately assign another task or project enabling the person to achieve recognizable results and satisfaction. Be sensitive to the fragility of confidence. Once people lose confidence in themselves, their performance, attitude, and potential drop alarmingly. Part of your job as a leader is to bolster that confidence so consistent achievement and job satisfaction can be achieved.

Use "we" rather than "you" when discussing the insufficient performance and possible solutions. Give your delegate a second chance to correct the problem(s) and achieve the desired results. Work along with your teammate to build self esteem, skills, and that all-important sense of confidence.

Because of the corporate cultures in many organizations, an employee may show reluctance, or even resistance, to accept responsibility beyond that already assigned as part of normal job duties. If you encounter that kind of response, move slowly and deliberately. Be sensitive to the feelings, perceptions, and motivations of your people.

Be sure that your expectation is reasonable and comfortable for the delegate. If that is not the case, look deeper. It may be that your assignment is, in reality, inappropriate for the employee. Are you attempting to delegate a distasteful task because you don't want to do it? It's likely that your employee will feel the same way. Delegate, don't dump.

Remember that you and your delegate(s) are members of the same team. You have a leadership role, making you a little bit different, but you still should be focused on achieving the same results. That shared focus can be used as a means of encouraging your people to work with you to get the job done. Working with your team members means performing the unpleasant as well as the pleasant tasks together. In basic terms, it means getting your hands dirty when your help is needed. Work together to achieve results.

Accountability

To build a successful organization of productive, proud, satisfied employees, emphasize accountability. It's not just for those in management; accountability is for everyone. The lower you "push" accountability in your organization, the more effective and involved your people will be.

Seek ways to heighten feelings of personal accountability on the part of each and every employee. Help everyone understand what is expected, and when, and that you hold each person accountable for fulfilling his or her part of the task. When each person meets those expectations, those accountabilities, three things will happen:

1. Each employee will have earned a sense of making a personal significant contribution to the group effort, a real sense of pride and satisfaction;
2. You, as a leader, will be developing your people and

accomplishing the objectives expected of your team by *your* leader; and

3. The organization will fulfill its goals as a consequence of everyone pulling together to get the job done as a team.

Be demanding of your people, in a firm and positive way. Set their sights high and assist them in the achievement of tasks they might have thought were beyond their capabilities. Be enthusiastic with your support, emphasizing shared responsibilities and personal accountability to self, co-workers, you as leader, and the organization.

Create a feeling of personal achievement, support, and focus on team goals, and people will gradually begin to assume more and more initiative. It probably won't just happen by itself; you have to clear the path so people feel comfortable doing things on their own. That's part of your job as an excelling leader.

Thought-Provoking Questions

1. It is said that people don't take enough initiative in their work. How do you feel about this allegation? What can you do to encourage people to show more initiative and accept more responsibility?
2. How is accountability defined in your organization? Do front line employees feel a sense of accountability? Why, or why not?
3. Do you and your people know when you're doing a good job? What are your criteria for that measurement?
4. How can delegation help you and your people excel?

Reader's Notes

9

Know Your People

By definition, you can't be a leader without followers. True followers are people who follow your lead because they believe in you and what you represent. Your relationships with others influence the degree to which they will follow you. So, we know that strong relationships are a key to excelling leadership.

To be a successful leader, it is essential to build positive relationships with the people around you. These other players in your game include your subordinates, of course, but also include superiors, peers, customers, suppliers, and people from other departments and companies. The rich, mutually-constructive relationships that support your success evolve from in-depth understandings about who people are, how they think, how they feel, how they act . . . and why.

As you build relationships with the significant people in your life—at work, at home, in school, in the community, in your trade or profession, you participate in a valuable sharing. You share ideas, ethics, beliefs, perspectives, experiences, goals, and visions. Through this open interchange, you establish—and maintain—a closeness that solidifies your relationships. The process of establishing and maintaining bonds between you and others may be described as networking, partnering, collaborating, teaming, and with similar terms that represent a deliberate coming-together.

Excelling leaders characteristically work closely with other people. To perform a leadership role effectively, you have to know those other people and they have to know you. You all have to work cooperatively as a team. You have to work together because you want to, not just because you have to.

There are several things you can do to get to know your people better. While you are getting to know them better, you'll also be letting them know more about you, your motivations, and how they can work best with you. Through a process of disclosure and feedback you'll gain invaluable understandings that will serve everyone involved positively.

The first thing you can do is easy: talk with your people. Find out more about why they are working for your organization. Notice the use of the word "with" instead of "at." This relationship is a consciously shared effort; doing things with others is more effective. Here is a partial list of things you might want to know:

- What kinds of work have they done before? What did they like best about their previous jobs? What did they like least? What kind of work would they like to do?
- What dreams and aspirations do they have for the future? How do they perceive their career development? How can you help them with this process?
- How do they feel about their jobs now? What would they like to do differently? Why? How would they go about it?
- What improvements would they like to see in the workplace? Why? How do they see your role in bringing about these improvements? How do they see their roles?
- What do your team members do when they're not at

work? What leadership positions have they held in volunteer organizations, church groups, and similar community activities?

- What are your team members most proud of, considering all their accomplishments over the years?

Family relationships and activities are very important to some of your team members. Some people prefer to keep their private lives separate from work; others are very open and want to share what's happening with their family or personal lives. As you come to know your people, you will learn who is comfortable sharing personal information and who is not. Be sensitive to their preferences. Listen, share, support, but don't pry.

To build relationships with your team members, share similar information with them about you, your background, interests, and family. Learn about each other, genuinely. Let them see that you are also a sensitive, caring human being, not just "the boss."

As you get to know your team members better, you'll discover more insights about their strengths and weaknesses. In conversations, they will build a higher level of authentic trust. They'll share with you the kind of work they like to do, and what they prefer not to do; when and where they like to work and who they prefer to work with. This knowledge can guide you in making your task assignments: people perform better those tasks they enjoy doing, along with those co-workers they enjoy being around.

Learning more about your people will inspire you to respect them as individuals. You will learn to genuinely appreciate what wonderful people you have on your team. They, in turn, will give you their support because of who you are and the way you treat them.

A favorite quotation applies here:

"People don't care how much you know until they know how much you care."

This homily has held true since first postulated by the ancient philosopher, Anonymous. Unfortunately, even though there's a lot of talk about the need for more caring in today's workplace, it still doesn't happen. Too many managers still take their power from their position, autocratic authority, and superior knowledge or information about where the company is going.

The process of getting to know your people is often a slow one. Some people will open up easily and will want to work with you for higher achievement. Others will be hesitant, reluctant to trust you—perhaps for quite a while. You'll have to prove yourself to them. Most of the people working with you will eventually communicate and become part of your team. Or, if they choose not to do so for some reason (and it will most likely be their reasons. not anything you do or don't do), they will leave or close their relationship with you of their own volition.

Some people working for you may be highly resistant to your teamwork/high achievement approach. For various reasons, stemming from the way they were raised, societal values, peer relationships, or organizational culture, they may fight you every step of the way. You may perceive some people as simply being "losers". That description is not necessarily true. They may not do everything you want them to do, but instead will do something they want to do. Their independence does not make them losers, but merely non-conformists. This attitude and behavior is certainly not all bad.

Everyone has some good qualities. Part of your job as their manager, as their leader, is to help bring out the positive values they can contribute to your shared effort. You may invest a considerable amount of time before discovering what motivates a recalcitrant employee. You'll have to make a decision, somewhere along the way, as to whether or not this person is worth the investment of your time and energies.

Since every situation is different, this book cannot offer a simple measurement for determining how long to work with a resistant employee before taking disciplinary action. To protect yourself under the process of administrative law, your best approach would probably be to work positively with each employee, documenting your efforts and administering formal discipline when appropriate.

Try to treat each employee individually, and on an adult-to-adult level. Look for the cause of the individual's behavior, and communicate openly. While you may be rebuffed, and more than once, you won't "break through" unless you keep trying. In some cases, matter-of-fact direct communication may be most appropriate; in other cases, you may be more successful with more feeling, more emotion.

Some people speak—and hear—on an intellectual level. Others are more heart-oriented, more feeling. As you get to know your team members, you will discover their preferences and proclivities. Respond to them in kind. If someone desires "heart" communication, you can talk all day from your "head" perspective and you probably won't ever "connect." The opposite applies, too, of course.

Each situation is different, so carefully consider all aspects, then move forward with positive determination. Remember also, your other team members are observing how you handle people who aren't pulling their weight. Letting someone "get by" may bring everyone's performance down to that lowest level. You'll be teaching them that a lower level of performance is just fine, dampening their internal drive to do better. Allowing performance and attitudes to atrophy to the lower levels will tacitly reinforce the substandard behavior.

Avoid discipline and it sends the same message as condoning the substandard behavior. Strong performers will soon wonder why they're working so hard when their efforts seem to exceed what their leader wants from them! If you don't pay attention . . . respect to their work, they'll soon adapt the lower level of performance or move on to another organization where they are more appreciated.

Understanding Human Behavior

A way you can learn more about your behavior style and that of each of your people is through a valid self-assessment learning instrument. The insight and information you gather will be highly valuable, since you'll discover why some people "tick" differently than others. Knowing something about the behavioral styles of the people on your team will enable you and your fellow team members to work even more effectively together. You'll have a greater appreciation of why and how your team members work individually and together.

Based on their behavioral style, people often prefer one kind of work over another. They will work differently with other kinds of people. With sufficient knowledge in this area, you can build teams of people with a balance of behavioral styles, and know how to best lead them to high achievement.

Seminars, courses, books, and magazine articles offer you as a leader further insight into human behavior, managerial styles, and various approaches to working most effectively with other people. Strive to expand your understanding of how you can best work with people. You can never learn enough in this important aspect of leadership.

Even with all the research and writing that has been done in the field of human motivation, it is clearly recognized that people do things for their reasons, not for yours. Your role as a leader is to create the right kind of environment for your people to excel. Much of that environment is created and influenced by the way you understand and work with your people.

One of the most widely-used valid behavioral styles learning instruments is the Personal Profile System available from Carlson Learning Companies. For information on this tool for increased understanding, contact the author by calling Herman Associates, Inc., at (800) 227-3566 or through his internet address, roger@herman.net.

More and more organizations are using 360-degree assessments to evaluate performance and productive work relationships. This process gathers input, using a questionnaire, from the person (manager, salesman, executive, and others) on his/her own effectiveness. Identical questions are asked of the subject's superior, peers, and subordinates, producing a comprehensive perspective of the subject individual. [When salespeople are evaluated, customers are invited to contribute their perceptions, as well.] While some in-house administration of such surveys is done, most organizations use independent outside consultants to assure objectivity and sensitivity.

The real value of 360-degree assessments is the processing of the information gathered, and the constructive action that is taken as a result of the learnings. We use several comprehensive assessment instruments and methodologies in our consulting work with all kinds of organizations who want to apply this technology. The key, though, is the commitment to use the knowledge productively . . . to make a positive difference that will be measured in concrete results.

To strengthen your leadership effectiveness, you can apply a powerful low-technology method that really works. If your people trust you . . . and if you trust them. Simple as it seems, just talk with people. Really. It's almost a lost art because we're all supposedly too busy these days. Just talk with people. Peers. Colleagues. Employees. Team members. Superiors. Customers. Suppliers. Family. Friends. Let these special people in your life know that you want to improve what you're doing in your life.

Genuinely solicit their input. Regard each of these folks as key members of your own personal Board of Advisors. Value their contributions to your success, as if you were paying them bags of gold for their observations and advice. In a sense, you are rewarding them handsomely, because their information is invaluable. These are people who, in all likelihood, really care about you. Their actual reward will come in watching you take their advice to heart and make significant improvements in your life. Chances are, many of them will become indirect (or even direct) benefactors of your enhanced effectiveness.

Now, here's the real power. As you reveal your vulnerability, seeking and accepting their support, they will become more comfortable in opening themselves to you. On a whole new level, you will begin to really know—much more than you ever have—those special people in your life. This openness will actually attract other people to open themselves to you, creating enriched understandings of each other. Imagine how such open and trusting relationships can help you achieve your life goals. And how you can support others in the achievement of what's important to them.

Employee Attitudes

Job performance is influenced by the attitudes your people have toward their work, their manager, their employer, and the customer. It's smart business to do everything you can to encourage positive attitudes. People's attitudes are influenced by the way they're treated . . . by you and by the total organization.

Remember, people behave based on their perceptions of what's happening around them; those perceptions may vary from reality.

There are three ways you can gain a deeper understanding of your team members' attitudes toward their work environment. One is to ask them. If you have a close relationship with your people, your open lines of communication will provide you with valuable information.

A second way to judge employee's attitudes is to watch people in their work environment. Attitude is often demonstrated by the way people do their work, their efforts to keep their work area clean and their equipment maintained, and by their interactions with you and other team members. These activities can serve as indicators for you. Watch for their facial expressions and body language. Use your intuition.

Just being alert to feelings and behaviors will put you in a stronger position.

A third way to assess those attitudes is through the use of an employee attitude survey. While this can be done in-house, perhaps by your human resources department, many organizations bring in outside consultants to conduct the survey, interpret the results, and provide an oral and/or written report to management and usually the team members themselves. My consulting firm does a lot of this kind of work and our clients have found it constructively revealing. People often have deep-seated and influential attitudes that won't be revealed in ordinary conversation or even interviews. Positive and negative feelings are often more easily expressed through paper and pencil (or computer interface) methods.

Employee attitudes will include desires and fears. As a leader, recognize that both emotions exist in the minds and hearts of each of your team members.

In the area of desires, everyone seeks to fulfill his or her own wants and needs. People have varying needs for achievement, freedom, security, responsibility, stability, personal contact with others, and standardized work procedures. Based on their personal situations, each of your team members will have a variety of other needs, including such things as increased income and time off. The more you learn about your people's needs, the more you can strive actively to meet those needs.

Employees also have fears. Some relate to the concerns presented in the previous paragraph. Other fears involve getting too close, too friendly, with the boss. Historically, many people have perceived that the boss is an adversary. If they have this sort of attitude, from personal or vicarious experiences, it will be difficult for some of your people to be receptive and cooperative to your excelling leadership style. When you encounter opposition generated by this fear, seek ways to demonstrate your sincerity and team-excelling attitude.

Some people have a get-by attitude that argues against striving for higher achievement. Low level, mediocre performance may have been learned as a value in the workplace. The get-by people may be afraid to try harder, perhaps because of fear of failure. Sometimes it's fear of punishment for not meeting standards or of damaged peer relationships. These uncertain people need special encouragement from you to break out of this all-too-comfortable perspective on life.

Fear of success also can inhibit performance. People who aren't fully confident of their abilities, or who are unsure of their capacity to behave appropriately when successful, will deliberately avoid performing at their highest level of capability. Special personal encouragement is needed by these people, too, to help them overcome and deal with their fears. Your people need your support, on an individual and personal level.

You may have a number of team members who will view the style described in this book with a great deal of suspicion. Turning things around in your organization could take quite a while, but it's probably still possible. The biggest obstacle to success is allowing negative attitudes to dampen enthusiasm and performance. Beware of peer pressure that might influence the people with whom you want to collaborate. That pressure could come from their subordinates, managers, and even peers. Some people might really want to cooperate with you, but are concerned about how others might react to their involvement.

Supporting Your People

A number of the people working for your organization may be involved in community organizations ranging from service clubs to Little League to Scouting groups to local volunteer fire departments. Or they may be active in Rotary, Kiwanis, the garden club, a newcomers group, or 4-H. The list goes on. These dedicated people invest a considerable amount of time and effort into these community service endeavors.

Some companies support their employees' involvement

by offering financial or other resources to help the organization their employees serve. Distribution of resources can be made in a number of ways. If not carefully controlled, however, this kind of program can get out of hand very easily. Every charitable organization seems to have its hand out for support in some way. A budget should be established, coordinated by a committee of company employees representing all levels of the organization (another opportunity for employee involvement). Reviewing opportunities to support local groups, the committee could prepare a set of recommendations for final decision-making consideration by the appropriate top management representative(s).

A more creative approach, putting more power in the hands of each individual employee, is to allocate your charitable contributions budget directly to your employees. Empower your employees to guide your company's community support. Let's see how this might work. First, divide your annual contributions budget by the number of people you employ. Allocate that per-person amount specifically to each employee. Ask each employee to decide, during the year, how to allocate his/her contribution on behalf of the company. The employee is free to donate his/her portion to any group or cause in the community that is not controversial or that might embarrass the company. This powerful practice enables employees to enhance their relationship with causes that are important to them . . . as members of your team.

Imagine one of your employees sitting around the kitchen table with other leaders of a community organization. They're bemoaning their need for funds for some worthwhile project, contemplating bake sales, car washes, raffles, or other ways to raise the money they need. Your employee volunteers that his/her employer will donate a certain amount to support the cause (whatever you have allocated per employee). How do you think the folks around the table feel toward your company and your employee? Even more important, how does your employee feel??

Your people are your organization's most important resource. Demographic shifts and other trends are gradually shifting our economy from a buyer's market to a seller's market for employees. We're already seeing the beginnings of a serious shortage of qualified workers. Employees will be in a position where they can be much more choosy about where they work. Companies are going to have to compete more for the top quality employees they desire. This means that the companies that are doing things right will be able to attract the best talent. The companies that earn a reputation for poor leadership will find it increasingly difficult to recruit the workers they need to serve their (internal and external) customers. For more information about this critical trend, read Turbulence!, my fifth book.

Now is the time to get your house in order. Your reputation for the way you work with your people could make a dramatic difference in the kinds of employees you will be able to attract and keep in a competitive marketplace.

Thought-Provoking Questions

1. How does knowledge of a team member's background and values help you excel as a leader?
2. If an employee doesn't "go along with the program", what can you do? How do you evaluate your alternatives to determine what actions to take?
3. Why should some of your organization's resources be invested to support community activities? How can this effort demonstrate support of your people?

Reader's Notes

Inspiration
and Support

To be effective as an excelling manager, your style of working with people must be different than the approach most prevalently used by traditional heavy-handed bossy managers.

Management philosophies are changing. The directive style is being replaced by a style in which the manager, as a leader and facilitator of high achievement, enables subordinates to perform and gives them inspiration and support to help them accomplish their tasks.

To better understand this concept, let's consider for a moment the "traditional" management approach that has been practiced for generations. The supervisor or manager has been recognized as "the boss," and "what the boss says goes." It's a directive style, with the manager telling subordinates what to do and expecting them to follow orders as given.

There is little concern for people's preferences, creative ideas, or personal growth under this philosophy. Most communication flows from the boss to the worker, with little input solicited or expected from the people on the front line. The focus of the work group is more on activities and specific tasks to be accomplished, rather than on results or how employees fit into the overall organization.

People working in the environment fostered by this style of management do things because they have to, not necessarily because they want to. Employees do (only) what they are told to do and are expected to accept current procedures as the most effective or productive approach. There is little, if any, encouragement for employees to become involved in improving how the organization operates.

Amazingly, this antiquated style is still prevalent in many organizations. The "experienced" managers were taught the autocratic style repeatedly over the years and directive, in-control, performance was positively reinforced by equally unenlightened executives and owners. It's genuinely difficult for such managers to break the old, comfortable habits. Many of them want to shift into the more modern, more appropriate styles, but honestly don't know how to make the change. They don't know how to lead without managing.

A wide variety of less autocratic management styles has been applied by executives, managers, and even entire companies. Many of these innovations were designed to give the worker more feeling of involvement in the boss's decisions. Unfortunately, most of these attempts gravitated to the "good buddy" system, where the manager and subordinate were supposed to be friends. In spite of the efforts to build more collaborative relationships, the boss was still the boss and whatever the boss said, went.

Leadership

A more successful philosophy suggests that a manager is

a leader. Management responsibilities, authority, and accountability remain, but they are applied in a different way. The manager guides, supports, and encourages people, rather than directing them to accomplish step-by-step assigned work. Clear expectations are negotiated, people are trained in how to accomplish the tasks, and are given the resources to do what is expected of them.

In a nutshell, the enlightened leader's job is to provide the physical and inspirational support to enable people to perform at their maximum potential. As a leader, your mission is to fully empower the wonderful, highly-talented people who work with you.

The old approach was to push people to get the job done, but as former President Dwight D. Eisenhower said, "You can't push a piece of string. You pull it." Leadership is a "come on, let's get it done" approach, rather than a "you do it" approach. Leaders encourage their followers to set their sights high, help clarify those goals and the methods by which they will be achieved, provide the needed resources, then get out of the way.

That last sentence is one of those expressions that bears repeating. Let's emphasize it by learning again that our role as leaders is to encourage our followers to set their sights high, help clarify those goals and the methods by which they will be achieved, provide the needed resources, then get out of their way.

The excelling leader gives team members freedom to do their work. He/she deliberately avoids looking over people's shoulders all the time, like a vulture watching for someone to make a mistake.

The leader is present and available, but with a different attitude. His/her presence is focused on inspiring the subordinate to perform at the highest level possible. This high productivity is accomplished through a solid relationship of trust and teamwork with the manager supporting individual achievement and the team's objectives.

This kind of leadership involves open communication. Team members must feel comfortable approaching their leader with problems, needs, ideas, and requests. Provide your subordinates with feedback on their effort, showing how their results contribute to the progress of the organization. Lead by example by showing that you are personally highly motivated. Show that you are enthusiastic about your work, and that you achieve results.

You can stimulate open communication, and convey a feeling of support by asking your team members what they need to give you their best performance. Ask your people, "What do you need from me in order to get your job done?" Appreciate that this new style will take a while for people to get used to.

Most employees are accustomed to bosses telling them what to do, rather than giving them the opportunity for input, decision-making authority, and personal responsibility. Be patient as you change your style and help your team members to change theirs.

Inspiration

Part of your mission as an excelling manager is to inspire your people to reach for their highest level of achievement. This level of effort is unique to the individual, because each person has different capabilities and interests. Your challenge is to bring out the best in each of your team members. Here are some things you can do:

1. Have Faith.

Believe in your people and their ability to perform at high levels. Take a personal interest in your team members. Become familiar with their knowledge, skills, abilities, talents, and interests. Think highly of your people and reflect that feeling in everything you do and say, whether your people are nearby or not.

2. Reflect Them.

Act as a mirror and help your workers see their individual strengths. Emphasize the positive things they contribute to the work environment. When looking at negative aspects or weaknesses, orient yourself and your employees toward personal improvement.

Seek to build the self-esteem of your people, showing each one's value to your organization. Work closely with them to set their sights progressively higher and higher. Help them build their positive attitudes toward themselves, their work, and their employer.

3. Nurture Them.

Help your people to grow in their work environment. Show them how to do the tasks you expect them to do. Together seek better ways to get things done. Enable them to learn new skills, new jobs, and new techniques to strengthen their personal value and their value to the organization. Praise them when they perform well and assure them that your criticism is constructive.

4. Insulate Them.

While you are spreading positive growth and achievement messages to your people, they will still be bombarded by conflicting messages of negativism and mediocrity. As much as you can, protect them from those conflicting messages until they are strongly enough rooted in the new design to ignore self-defeating messages.

Help them keep things in perspective, realizing that even though they are striving to excel they may still be surrounded by mediocrity in various forms. Respect and support their efforts to strive to excel in what they are doing. They are making a difference; even small contributions strengthen the overall picture.

5. Encourage Independence.

Seek ways to individualize the responsibility assigned to each of your people. Enable them to see the results of their independent efforts, even though they are working as part of a team. You want to build a team feeling, but each member of the team also must appreciate his/her personal contribution to the final results being achieved.

Along with encouraging independence and personal accountability, be receptive to innovation. There will always be new, different, and often better ways to do things. The greatest source of these ideas is the person actually performing the work. Ask each of these people closest to the action for ideas on how to improve the way things are being done.

Just asking occasionally will keep your people alert for new methods. Encouraging response will reinforce your interest in having their input. Receive their ideas appreciatively and enthusiastically. Be sure to provide feedback so your people will know what you have done with their contributions.

6. Set the Example.

Your team members will look to you as their leader to set the pace for the team. If you are lethargic, you can expect the same from them. If you are energetic and enthusiastic, you'll receive more of that behavior in return from your people.

Demonstrate your positive mental attitude; if you've got problems, don't let your frustration or irritation be perceived by your people. Attitudes, both positive and negative, are contagious in the workplace.

Your people will observe the way you do your job. If they see you are organized, goal-directed, and results-oriented, they will be positively impressed. Demonstrate that you plan your work, perform your work deliberately, and follow-through on the details. People like to follow a leader who knows the path to success and shows competence, confidence, and high achievement on the job.

Support

There are a number of ways to support your people to help them excel. Obvious methods include ensuring that they have the tools, equipment, and other resources to get the job done. Keep their incoming work flowing smoothly and at a pace that is comfortable, yet challenging. Give your people a good working environment, including sufficient space, light, and sound control to encourage high performance. Directly or indirectly, provide technical expertise and support for your team members as they need it.

Your personal moral support will be a positive factor. In appropriate ways, cheer your people on as a good sports team coach would do. Expect high achievement, be firm, yet work cooperatively with them to help them excel. As they assume more responsibility and accountability for their own performance, help them overcome their fears of uncertainty and insecurity. Build their confidence by expressing your confidence in them.

Enable formation and functioning of support groups in the workplace. Your people can learn and grow through their relationships with others who can serve as a sounding board for ideas, offer suggestions on how to improve, and provide peer group moral support. Consider forming your own support group with fellow managers to discuss approaches to solving problems and enhancing growth.

As long as your work group still meets or surpasses its objectives, be receptive to doing things different ways. Your team members have valuable ideas about changing job assignments, work methods, work flow, and other aspects of their environment. Give them the "space" to try their new approaches. Appreciate that being close to the action gives them perspectives you don't have at your leadership level. It is different.

For example, an increasing number of organizations are adopting a concept known as "flex time". Within legitimate constraints based on when certain jobs have to be done, employees are permitted to come in early and leave early, or come in later and leave later.

This flexibility is sincerely appreciated by working parents who have to get children off to school and meet them after school. It helps in the operation of car pools and scheduling of personal matters such as health care appointments. And, of course, there are those who like to sleep late and there are those who are early risers.

The more you can do to respond to the needs and desires of your team members, the more productive they will be. What you're trying to do is create and maintain a work environment that is most conducive to high productivity and worker satisfaction.

Your people will perform at higher levels if you, as their caring manager, inspire them to that excelling achievement. People naturally want to do a good job, so give them the support they need to do it.

Your employees are human beings with all sorts of emotions that can affect their work. Be sensitive to those emotions and appreciate the individuality of each person working with you. Encourage them to do their best, but accept the fact that they may make mistakes. Let them know you understand they aren't perfect. You can also make mistakes. Your key concern should not be whether mistakes are made, but what you can learn from them and how you can assure that desired results are still achieved.

Response to mistakes should be tolerant, understanding and supportive, or people will be afraid to try anything on their own. When you discover a mistake, put it in perspective. Determine the real and potential impact of the mistake and take steps to reduce or eliminate the negative outcomes. Do what you can to prevent the mistake from happening again, then move forward to achieve more progress in your work.

Don't just fix mistakes with an attitude that the organization couldn't exist without you to solve the problems. Instead, actively and eagerly involve the workers in the improvement or correction process. Instead of making people wrong with destructive finger-pointing, you'll work together to gain the wonderful feeling of having met and overcome a challenge.

Blame will be merely punative. It won't solve the problem and it won't keep in from happening again.

Thought-Provoking Questions

1. Can managers practice supportive leadership approaches and still be "in control"?
2. How can a manager shift his/her style from a directive to a supportive orientation? What will convey this change to others?
3. Describe how an excelling manager leads by example.

Reader's Notes

Involvement

Survey after survey confirms that one of the strongest motivators of employee performance and satisfaction is "involvement". People want to be involved in their work organization. They want an opportunity for input into what happens at work, particularly when it affects their own job. They want more control over their destiny.

Helping your people become more involved, in legitimate and significant ways, is fully consistent with building an excelling organization. The more positive involvement your employees feel, the more they will be committed to personal and team high achievement. They will have a part in the organization, a vested interest, a sense of ownership. This kind of feeling builds dedicated high performance, productivity, and loyalty.

How to Do It

There are a number of ways you can enable your subordinates to increase their level of involvement in your company. They can voluntarily join, or be appointed to, committees, task forces, study groups, or special project teams within work groups or on an organization-wide basis. These kinds of groups are active, in many organizations, in coordinating employee suggestion systems, product development, worker safety programs, work methods improvement, and even corporate strategic direction.

You can encourage your people to become involved with organization-based groups coordinating company picnics, United Way fund raising, and company-sponsored sports teams. Such involvement will strengthen their feeling of belonging to the organization, making a difference. Consider also business-related involvement opportunities outside the company environment. Examples include representing the employer on Chamber of Commerce committees or similar involvement with industry trade associations. Such outside activities also offer wonderful opportunities for leadership development.

Involve your people in ways that will give each employee more real control over work expectations, increasing the sense of accountability for personal performance. When true accountability increases, so do productivity, results, and quality.

Shared Job Design

The first opportunity for involvement is the design (or re-design) of the employees' jobs, how the jobs should be done, and what specific performance results are expected. In some cases, employees may be able to help write or re-write the job description for their positions. Encourage employees to discuss with you your mutual perceptions of the job and the best way to accomplish the work. Not only with the resultant job description be much more legitimate, commitment to performance will be demonstrably higher. Keep job descriptions fluid, encouraging people to modify them as they discover new and better ways to accomplish the work of the organization.

As goals and objectives are developed for your organization, your team members should have input into setting the operational result targets for their own departments or work groups. Explain what overall results are expected of the larger group, then let the workers (who are closest to the work) consider alternative methods for getting the job done. This approach reduces your personal work load in making assignments, gives your people some control over how things are done, and may well result in a better use of available resources.

If people are given a chance to show what they can really produce, their achievement is often better than what may have been expected by people outside the work group—including bosses and stopwatch-toting industrial engineers. Give your dedicated employees the opportunity to set high performance goals for themselves, then demonstrate their capability for high achievement. There is significantly more chance that the expectations will be met because the employees are setting goals for themselves. An old saw applies to this scenario: "People support what they help to create."

The concept of people having this kind of input and control is called "ownership". Those involved automatically assume responsibility and accountability for their work. Give them the opportunity to create their own job expectations, within the constraints of meeting the objectives of your work group and the organization. Give them control over the various aspects of the work, with all the resources they need to succeed. Now they "own" the process . . . and the results.

This concept of ownership can apply to other aspects of the employee's life in the workplace. Give your employees responsibility for their own work area. Seek ways to enhance your employees' feeling of personal involvement in their work and work environment. Most people want this kind of personal linkage with their work. They need to feel that part of the workplace "belongs" to them. Personal items in offices are an example of how people can build their own identities with their performance on the job.

I am constantly amazed as, even today, I encounter companies that have rules against putting personal items (like family photos) at work stations. People like to have personal things like pictures, plants, coffee mugs, posters, and knickknacks around them. It's humanizing and it's fun. If you tell employees they are not permitted to have these personal treasures, these simple pleasures, then you send a very clear message: there are two parts of life: fun and enjoyment . . . and work. When work ceases to have an enjoyable component, employee motivation drops like a rock. The work environment becomes a place where workers would rather not be. Not a very productive scenario, is it?

As the employees perform on the job, creatively seek other ways to build involvement and ownership. If a report is prepared by one or more employees, whether for internal or external consumption, include in the report recognition by name for the employee(s) who had a part in its design and production. Having people share the rewards and the pride of accomplishment can be powerfully productive.

When problems arise in your team's area of responsibility, don't try to solve them yourself. Of course, as a manager/leader, you have the responsibility for solving problems and making necessary decisions. But, whenever possible, share problems with your team members, individually or as a group, and ask for their input. People like to help solve work group problems, particularly as the solutions may affect their work. As they assume greater involvement in the identification and solution of problems (even before they occur), your managerial problem-solving role will diminish. Watch how much more time you have for your other responsibilities!

In one of my client companies, a decision was made to increase inventory levels in a particular department. The manager had to decide how to redesign use of the available storage space. After thinking of several equally appropriate alternatives, she asked the advice of her team members. Several of them put their heads together and constructed a solution that was better than any of those developed by the manager. Their daily use of the inventory storage system gave them a practical insight the manager didn't have.

Another way to build involvement is to have regular meetings with your work group. Share with them information about what's happening in the organization and how the work group might be affected. Discuss what's been happening in the work group, asking members to report on their own activities. Include a "comments for the good of the work group" period when anyone can raise questions or make suggestions or discuss how the group's performance can be improved.

As we've seen, there is value in encouraging employee suggestions about work methods, work flow, materials handling, job assignments, scheduling, and anything else that might apply to the way you operate. With their input, employees will not only be personally involved, but they will have some degree of impact on their own work. Their influence on their work will reduce the necessity for you to be so involved with aspects they can handle just fine. Gradually, the evolution to greater autonomy will make your work easier and more productive as their leader.

Performance Appraisal Partnerships

The second opportunity for significant employee involvement is participation in the performance appraisal process. You can even "contract" with the employee about what behaviors or performance will be evaluated, as well as the criteria to be used for measurement.

Traditionally, performance appraisal forms are completed by the manager on an annual or semi-annual basis. The manager then calls the employee in for the evaluation interview and tells the employee what kind of performance scores are being submitted. This is a one-way communication approach. The only input the employee has is to sign the form, agreeing with the evaluation or indicating disagreement with the manager's perception.

Engage your employees in the performance appraisal process, building involvement, communication, accountability, and ownership . . . and probably a greater sense of reality. If you've worked with the employee in the design of the expectations of work to be performed, it's a natural and logical progression to have the employee involved in evaluating how well those expectations have been met.

Employee appraisals are handled in various ways in different organizations. In some cases, they are conducted annually, with all employees being evaluated at the same time. This schedule puts a real burden on the manager, because there is too little time to carefully consider individual performance and work personally with each employee. There is a natural tendency to compare one employee against another, even though that sort of comparison probably has no validity whatsoever in the actual measurement of a particular employee's performance. The heavy load, all coming at once, tacitly encourages managers to give the evaluations a white wash job and move on to the next task.

A better approach is to schedule the employee's appraisal based on the anniversary of the person's date of employment. Feeling that a full year is too long a period between formal evaluations, many organizations are switching to a semi-annual evaluation schedule.

Some are conducting quarterly appraisals to keep the knowledge and formal supervisor-subordinate communication about performance as current as possible.

If you are concerned about how to remember all those things your employees do between formal evaluations, try carrying a small notebook with you. Using a series of pages for each of your subordinates, record anything that might be appropriate to consider when completing the appraisal form. Be careful about making notations obviously, in view of your people. If not done carefully, people could develop a fear or hate, or at least suspicion, about the boss's little book. This sort of attitude is counterproductive and could easily breed a culture of fear and suspicion.

Whatever performance appraisal schedule is followed by your organization, the person or department responsible for coordinating the evaluation program probably sends you a note that it's time for you to rate a specific employee. Attached to the note is a standardized form for you to complete. If you're the initiator of the process, a calendar notation will assure that the assessment sequence is activated in a timely manner.

To involve the employee in this process, ask him/her to complete a copy of the blank appraisal form, as a self-evaluation of performance. Have the employee identify areas where improvement is needed or desired. What support is requested from the manager to help achieve those improvements? The employee's immediate supervisor also completes a copy of the same form, indicating his/her evaluation of the employee's performance.

When you and the employee meet for the appraisal interview, compare each other's perceptions of how the employee performed. As you discuss the evaluations that each of you has written, consideration of the similarities and/or differences in measurement will generate open communication between you. As you work together to resolve differences between your perceptions, you will produce a much more realistic assessment to submit for inclusion in the employee's personnel file. Make this appraisal a positive experience.

As part of this partnership approach to performance appraisal, you should consider ways the employee might improve performance on the present job and/or prepare to assume additional or more responsibilities in the future.

The appraisal interview process is also a wonderful opportunity to have the employee evaluate his/her supervisor. How good a job is the supervisor doing for the employee? What else would the employee like from the supervisor? Support? Training? Different communication? More clear expectations? When two-way evaluations are the rule, both parties become more accountable to each other. A partnership develops, instead of a you-vs.-me relationship. The attitude becomes "how can we help each other meet the other's expectations?"

Managers can be evaluated by their subordinates, peers, and supervisor using a 360-degree assessment. Even customers can become involved in this type of comprehensive appraisal of an individual's style, performance, and effectiveness. I have found the 360-degree tools, and their companion organizational culture surveys, to be very useful in the corporate arena.

In situations where a number of people work together, shared evaluations can be productive. A variety of techniques can be used to bring out how people feel about each other, the team, the work. Emphasis can be placed on positive aspects, but there are risks of hurt feelings, misinterpretations, and other problems when surveys (especially home-made) are applied by people who haven't been trained in the process of survey technology. In times like these, when so much could be at stake, that it may be wise to bring in an outside management consultant.

Professional Growth

Education, training, and development offer another powerful opportunity for employee involvement. Practically all employees want to grow, personally and professionally. They want to learn new techniques, understand wider perspectives, build stronger skills, comprehend larger systems, and gain greater insights. In short, they want to equip themselves to be better tomorrow than they were yesterday . . . or even today!

Please note that growth is not necessarily devoted to raising one's position on the corporate organizational chart. A lot of workers would rather strengthen their capacity at their present level, rather than moving up into positions of higher power . . . and responsibility.

Since most growth is work-related, employees hold an expectation that their employer will provide—directly or indirectly—a variety of formal and informal learning opportunities. Workers at all levels and in all occupations want opportunities to gain knowledge and skills that will help them maximize their career options, as well as do an even better job for their current employers. With the confidence that they can easily shift employers, workers display a different attitude toward their current positions. They're there because they want to be, not because they are trapped by a lack of knowledge, skills, or experience.

This formal and informal learning can be acquired through such means as on-the-job training, in-house seminars and workshops, external seminars, university courses (both credit and non-credit), and conferences sponsored by trade associations and professional organizations. We'll soon see a vast array of learning opportunities offered electronically through the internet, as well. Given the global nature of this technology, there will be no limits on what knowledge can be acquired from sources throughout the world.

Together, you and the employee can design a schedule of on-the-job and formal training experiences for the employee's growth. Give your employees more control over their destiny through career planning and development. Have them wholly involved with the process, even though assignment relationships will be made by a seemingly disconnected "home office" somewhere.

Create for each employee under your leadership a plan of growth and development specifically tailored for that individual. Don't promise promotions, compensation increases, or job assignments. Those opportunities will be there, in all likelihood, for those who prepare for them, but promises made and unfulfilled—for whatever reason—create unhealthy feelings of distrust. As you help people prepare for their futures, you'll simultaneously encourage them to improve their current and short-term performance. They are positioning themselves to be able to take advantage of opportunities.

Participative Management

The concept of participative management encourages leaders to involve employees in the management of the organizational team. Everyone participates in the decision-making process in one way or another. All the employees involved feel a personal investment in the future of the organization. After all, they're directly involved in determining its success and future direction.

Participative management approaches have been tried in a wide variety of organizations with mixed success. While the concept is good in theory, sometimes it doesn't work so well in practice. Problems arise in two areas: how the system is designed and implemented in the company, and reluctance on the part of the managers and/or other employees.

All the ideas discussed in this chapter will work if you apply them seriously and sincerely. Your purpose is to enable your people to become more legitimately involved in their work organization. Keep that focus clear. Provide opportunities for people to contribute their ideas, to influence the decisions that influence the design, scope, strategies, systems, and results of their employer.

Expect resistance from suspicious employees who are accustomed, after many years of living in this-is-the-way-we-do-things-here world. Work to overcome that resistance by showing consistent performance in reaching out for . . . and implementing new ideas or approaches. Create a safe place for people to get involved, to see the benefit of their involvement (things actually happening), and to feel appreciated for their involvement.

The manager of a medium-sized machine shop wanted more production from his people. He gathered them together and explained his interest in hearing their ideas on improving productivity. They were suspicious of his talk about working as a team, since he had always made every decision independently. Deciding to give the participative approach a chance, they began making suggestions and requests.

Rather than being receptive to all their ideas, the superintendent implemented ideas he liked and ridiculed those he didn't. He rarely gave credit to his subordinates for their input. Before long, the production workers saw their boss' lack of commitment to real employee involvement. An adversary relationship developed, production dropped, and the superintendent was eventually replaced.

There are better ways to approach the implementation of participative leadership. The concepts presented in this book will give you a good grounding. Remember that your people want to be genuinely involved in your organization's success. Give them the opportunity to work together as a real team and you can accomplish amazing results. The rest is up to you!

Thought-Provoking Questions

1. How much do your employees really want to be involved with leadership and decision making? How do you know?
2. Can employees legitimately evaluate their own performance? Why, or why not?
3. How can you overcome employee reluctance to become more involved?

Reader's Notes

Feedback
and Recognition

People need and want constructive feedback. Most try to do a good job and want to know how they're doing. In spite of common beliefs, most employees want to excel in their work. They want to go home at the conclusion of their work day with a sense of satisfaction of having accomplished something, of having made a positive difference in the world.

In our research, we asked workers if they wanted to excel at work. Most (over 97 percent) said "yes," usually with some degree of enthusiasm. Next, we asked these same workers if they did excel at work. Most (over 82 percent in our ongoing research) responded "No." They openly admitted that they were not doing their best. The next logical question was why they were not doing their best. The responses came back in various forms of "My boss won't let me."

Now, I doubt that there are many bosses—at any level in any organization—who will implore people, "Don't work so hard! You'll make me look bad." That just wouldn't make sense. Yet, workers get this message from their leaders, and act accordingly. No, we don't send that kind of message deliberately, but people absorb that message because of what their leaders say and do . . . including what they don't say and don't do.

If there are ways they can improve, most people are receptive to learning about them. This desire will be most prevalent and productive when the feedback is given in a positive, constructive way, rather than destructive. Nobody likes to be criticized unfairly.

Help your subordinates see the positive aspects of their work. Compliment them on work well done. When their performance level or other behaviors need to be changed, show how the proposed changes will be an improvement. Genuinely seek to help your people improve. Be positive; don't pick on others, even in jest. The potential wounds may never heal, limiting the potential of the worker, the leader, and the team.

Some people are very sensitive about criticism, even though they may not manifest their feelings outwardly. Instead of emphasizing faults, focus instead on opportunities for growth. Maintain a consistent positive attitude.

More specifically, people want recognition when they deserve it. They want to be recognized by their peers and by their manager. That recognition is welcome in many forms, not just monetary rewards. Sometimes just a sincere "thank you" for their contribution to the work group's success is all that is really needed or wanted.

Even though it's so easy to do, many managers seem to have a problem complimenting others. Remember, your people want to feel appreciated for what they do. They don't want to be taken for granted.

Giving Feedback

Feedback is an ongoing activity. You do it all the time, consciously and unconsciously, with all your subordinates. It is not something to be done only during the formal annual performance appraisal. Unfortunately, in many organizations, the only time workers get feedback is during that official interview. Feedback should be a normal part of the communications process between you and everyone with whom you work, especially your team members.

The process starts when you assign tasks to your people. Be clear in your expectations; be sure your employee understands exactly what you want. Observe the employee's performance as the assignment is begun. If there are any difficulties, act promptly and supportively to resolve them.

Encourage each of your people on a regular, consistent, and honest basis. Praise their achievements, no matter how small. Coach each one personally to overcome any deficiencies in performance, with specific (measurable) suggestions wherever possible.

When someone has done something well, giving feedback is easy. Tell the person what you perceive and that you're pleased with what's been done. When appropriate, refer to your expectations and discuss how they've been met or exceeded. Again, your being specific makes the communication much more meaningful.

This approach helps the employee focus on his/her performance compared to your agreed-upon expectations for that performance. If your expectations were clear to the employee, your comments will serve as positive reinforcement of what the employee already knows has been achieved. If your expectations were not clear, your feedback will provide an opportunity for both critique and clarification.

While exceptional achievement should always be commended, well-done routine work should also be recognized.

Things like coming to work on time, keeping work materials neatly and safely stored, and maintaining a clean work area are "expected", but should be appreciated with some occasional feedback. Just a few words once in a while, to let employees know you have noticed and that you appreciate what they do, will be well-received.

Some of your employees may rarely do anything extraordinary, but they can be depended upon to get their assigned jobs done in a satisfactory, consistent manner. These people require and deserve recognition, too. Once in a while, just mention that you appreciate them being part of the team. Let them know your job is made easier because you can always depend on them. If you can find something specific to recognize, that's even better.

When employees are not doing what you expect, you need to give them realistic feedback. Don't be completely negative. Find something positive about what is being done, and mention that, too. Otherwise, it will seem like you're just looking for their bad performance. They'll resent your constant criticism, and so will their friends among your employees. Those negative feelings could erode your team cohesiveness.

Perhaps you have an employee who is turning out high quality work, but not enough of it. You can praise the work that is being done, while reminding the employee of your expectations for higher achievement. Don't just criticize the employee for not doing all you wish; find out why performance is lower than desired.

See if the employee can offer some suggestions about what can be done to improve performance. The problem may not be entirely the employee's fault. There may be things you can do to have a machine adjusted, increase the raw material supply, improve the lighting, or help the employee set priorities to accomplish results as desired.

Look carefully at every situation where an employee is not performing as you expect. Are the expectations clearly understood? Does the employee have sufficient training and experience to do what you ask? What about the employee's attitude toward work, you, or the organization? Are there distracting problems at home or personal health concerns?

Don't be too quick to criticize when performance is substandard. Look for the causes: that's what you have to address. Search for why you're not getting your desired results; look beneath the symptoms to discover the real problem. Solve the cause of the deficiency and you'll improve performance. If you merely address the symptoms of your problem, you may never see the change you want.

Your responsibility as manager is to call the employee's attention to the problem, work together to identify and understand the causes, then seek ways to correct the situation. Do what is appropriate for you to do, but place on the employee whatever responsibility rightfully belongs to him/her. Stay focused on the roles here: your role and the employee's role are separate and distinct.

Remember, you are holding that employee accountable for meeting the job expectations which you both agreed were legitimate. If you're not getting the results you desire, ask why. Don't overlook the possible need to adjust the expectations; they should be as realistic as possible.

Don't fall into the trap of letting things go for a while, hoping they'll improve. They usually don't. If discipline is called for, begin the process. Be consistent in the way you work with all your subordinates. Employees expect that everyone has a share of the load to carry, and each should do his/her part.

Low producers hurt the team, and you're the one who has to respond to the situation. You should have high expectations of everyone. Don't give special treatment to anyone; everyone else will legitimately interpret your action to mean that the rules have changed. They will assume that they, too, can now produce at the lower level.

All your feedback should be specific and sincere. Don't fall into the trap of giving someone a "whitewash job"—saying everything the employee does is just wonderful. Your team member will suspect that your comments are not genuine, so your words will be "empty."

After someone hears that he/she is terrific for a period of time, it is difficult to administer a more realistic appraisal in the future. Just tell it like it is. If you get a negative or resistive response from the employee, listen to discover why. Then respond to the causes of the resistance; don't try to respond only to the surface behavior.

Treat your people like adults. In many organizations, the relationship between the manager and the subordinate is best described as parent-to-child. Given today's values in the workplace, a more effective approach will be adult-to-adult.

A well-known rule of thumb that bears repeating is "praise publicly and criticize privately." Avoid giving people negative feedback where others can observe. Talk quietly or get the employee off somewhere where you can have some privacy for the discussion.

Sometimes your office can be intimidating for your subordinates, particularly if they're not used to going to your office for routine matters. Others may see an employee going into your office and assume that the person is being "called on the carpet." Either make your office a comfortable, well-used communications location, or seek some neutral location to counsel an employee with whom you have a problem.

As a manager, it is wise for you to seek feedback on your own performance. Whenever you feel you need it, ask your superior. Invite your subordinates to give you feedback on how you're doing your job. Ask them how well they feel you're supporting them. Don't react defensively if you hear something negative. Learn from the experience.Some of my greatest learnings as a leader came from my direct reports.

During the formal, written performance appraisal process, some enlightened companies are asking employees to complete a self-evaluation using the same form that the supervisor completes. The supervisor and subordinate then sit down and compare what they've written. If they've communicated well, with valid feedback on a constant basis, the rating should be fairly consistent.

This experience will help open more communication, clarifying expectations further and strengthening feedback. Each of you will have different perceptions of what/how results are being accomplished. This sharing is incredibly valuable in building cooperative positive work relationships.

Seek to understand the perception the other person has. Listen and learn. Don't be too quick to defend your position. Help your team member better understand what you expect. Be open to his/her opinions and ideas. If you receive some criticism, seek ways to correct your problem. Remember, part of your role as a manager is to meet the expectations your people have of you.

Using this same approach with your superior will enhance your understanding, strengthening the performance of you and your team.

Giving Recognition

There are a number of ways to give employees recognition for work well done. Money, of course, is always welcome. You can use money as a reward by increasing an employee's pay or giving a bonus or prize for exceptional performance. Remember that this activity, like so many others in the workplace, must be consistent.

If you give cash awards for high performance in one area or at one point in time, your people will expect it when those circumstances are present again. Be sure you are clear about how awards of this kind are judged and granted. It's best to have a well-understood, written, consistent program that is used throughout the organization.

There are a number of alternatives to cash rewards. Letters of commendation can be effective. Put a copy in the employee's personnel file; send the original home by mail. This will enable the employee's family to participate in the recognition. After the employee has received the letter, you might want to post a copy on the bulletin board to give the employee some public recognition of the achievement. Appreciation can also be expressed with a certificate or a plaque.

Another way to recognize employee performance is to give the employee a day off with pay. If possible, allow the employee to choose the day. Perhaps it could be added to time off around a holiday or vacation. Working parents appreciate a day off once in a while to catch up with off- the-job responsibilities. Some employees would enjoy a day off when entertaining out-of-town guests.

Getaway weekends are popular in some areas. This type of reward would be a particularly valuable recognition to an employee whose spouse also works. It would give them an opportunity to just get away together for a couple of days with at least part of their expenses paid. The same principle applies to a night out, say dinner and tickets to the theater or a special event, paid for by the employer. Consider including the cost of babysitters in the reward package.

A variation on this idea is for the manager and the manager's spouse to take the employee and the employee's spouse out for the evening. Or the manager could just take the employee to lunch. In some companies, senior managers routinely take employees, selected from a number of different departments, to lunch. The open discussion builds trust, helps disseminate information and attitudes, and provides an opportunity for off-the-record feedback to management. You'd be amazed at the sorts of issues that surface in those get-togethers, and the value of the information that is fed to the manager or executive.

Gift certificates for merchandise are always welcome. You can purchase gift certificates from many stores in your area. The employee earns a certain number of points for various achievements and can then turn in the points for desired merchandise.

Companies specializing in performance incentive programs emphasize that having a carefully developed system is the correct approach. Performance must be measurable and a legitimate reward program must be established. Employees earn points for various achievements, such as meeting or exceeding quotas or standards. Those points can be applied to merchandise shown in special catalogs, to vacation trips, or to cruises. The gift catalogs produced by incentive companies are usually marketed to company sales managers, but have applications far beyond the sales field.

The key difference between cash awards and non-cash incentive programs is the motivation attitude of the employee. Studies show that employees receiving cash usually use the money to meet family needs: orthodontia, painting the house, buying furniture, or paying bills. Those are things we "have" to do. Non-cash awards appeal to the "want- to" motivations. The benefits are things the winners can personally enjoy as something unusual, special, or otherwise unattainable.

Sending employees to seminars, conferences, or conventions can be a reward for good performance and also help employees learn and grow. As recognition for some performance or achievement, the organization pays the tuition and any other expenses for the worthy employee. You're rewarding good performance with the opportunity to learn more to improve effectiveness or position in the organization. This incentive is particularly valuable for employees who are active in their professional or trade organizations and want to attend their meetings.

A form of recognition that would be valuable to many of your employees is an opportunity to work on an innovative idea with company support. If someone has a good idea, enable that person to risk, to experiment, to see what can be developed. That kind of support gives special recognition to that employee. You're saying "we have faith in you", and that's pretty strong recognition to creative people eager to try new ways of doing things.

Whatever recognition you award should be legitimately deserved. The value of the reward should be consistent with the value of the employee's contribution or achievement. Be sure the employee also perceives your form of recognition as a real reward. Always document formal recognition in the employee's personnel file so there is a permanent record.

Thought-Provoking Questions

1. How do you give feedback to your people now? What results have you seen? What can you do, starting right away, to improve in this area?
2. Where do you draw the line between what an employee should do automatically and what should be praised as a noteworthy performance?
3. In what ways could feedback and recognition be used to energize so called "average" employees?
4. What mechanisms can you put in place to generate feedback on your performance?

Reader's Notes

13

Managing Priorities and Time

The management of priorities and time are vital skills for the excelling leader. Your strength in the effective application of these skills, will help you make a significant contribution to your organization . . . and to the people who look to you as a role model.

The real power in mastering these skills is two-fold. First, you'll learn time management and priority management yourself for your own use. Second, as an excelling leader, you'll help your people learn and practice these skills as well. As both you and your co-workers become more proficient in the use of these vital techniques, you will work together more effectively and more efficiently.

It's important to appreciate the distinction between efficiency and effectiveness. Efficiency has been described as doing things right; effectiveness means doing the right things. Both goals are worthy, and both should be pursued.

Check yourself frequently. Are you doing the things you should be doing to achieve your goals and objectives? How well are you performing those things you are doing? If you are doing the wrong things, it doesn't matter how well you are doing them. Doing the right things, and doing the most important things, is essential. Determining your priorities becomes of critical importance.

Once you're sure you have your priorities in order, focus on performing your tasks in the best way possible. If your priorities are not clear, even the sharpest time management skills will help achieve good results. When you gain the clarity in your goals and priorities, the mechanics of time management will play a major role. You'll be more organized, better planned, more deliberately focused, and more confident. Your success depends on how well you manage your time and the time of those working with you. Combine definitive goals and priorities with comfort with mechanical time management skills, you will be well-prepared for high performance.

Priority Management

Active leaders will always have too much to do. It's the nature of the world in which we live. Even when overwhelmed with projects and tasks to accomplish, it's easy to yield to the temptation of unexpected enticing opportunities that threaten to lead us off on time-consuming tangents. Being distracted is a normal human foible. You must consciously strive to maintain a clear focus on your mission and goals or you'll be hopping down rabbit trails chasing elusive dreams forever.

Of course, this clear focus means that you must have a rock-solid understanding of, and commitment to, your mission and personal responsibilities to fulfill that mission. You must know for what you are held accountable, and the relative importance of each of those objectives.

Establishing the relative importance of tasks is described

as "setting priorities". In considering all the work you have to do, you have to know what tasks or concerns take precedence over others. You should be able to list your responsibilities and rank them by level of importance.

Setting priorities seems simple enough, but surprisingly few leaders and supervisors do it consciously. In my years as a management consultant, I've been amazed at how many high level executives allow themselves to be led astray by capricious outside influences. Simple tasks sometimes require the greatest attention to assure their completion. Be careful: it's the little things that will "get" you!

You have the power to set most, if not all, of your priorities. Of course, there are certain aspects of your job that need to be done sooner than others. Some things just have to be accomplished before other work can be done. Listing these tasks or operations in rank order, by scheduling importance and/or sequence, is a significant part of actually setting priorities. Some priority-setting is practically automatic or second-nature; you are probably doing it already.

Some of your priorities will be influenced by what your superiors expect of you. These expectations should come from the organization's established mission, goals and objectives referred to earlier. Organizational priorities, determined strategically by top management, should strongly influence your priorities.

Your highest priorities should be those activities that will enable you to achieve your responsibilities in the accomplishment of the organization's mission. Focus your strongest energies on your mission-oriented tasks, and let everything else fall to a lower priority. If you have a clear idea of what your leadership expects from you, establishing these priorities is easy to do. If you are confused about what your superiors expect—where they place their priorities, you'll be operating in a dangerous vacuum. Get higher level answers first, then you can more legitimately set your own priorities to support the organizational design.

Part of your responsibility as a leader is to help your subordinates set their priorities. The foundation of this work is clarification of your expectations of them. Their priorities should flow from your priorities, and consequently support achievement of the overall organizational plan. Help them understand and appreciate the connection between what they do and what you do. Show them conclusively how they fit into the "big picture" . . . and how the "big picture" influences their work.

Let your people know what you consider most important—in terms of tasks demanding attention and results that must be achieved by particular times. Keep them informed about shifting organizational priorities. Share priorities of all members of your team with everyone else on your team. Understanding what others are striving to do helps everyone manage his/her resources better.

Commit your priorities to writing to strengthen that understanding. Encourage your people to commit their priorities to writing, also, enabling them to better visualize what needs to be done. Keep them abreast of any deadlines that affect them, as well as any changes in company strategy, the marketplace environment, available resources, and similar factors that may influence their work. Maintain sensitivity to the relationships between their work and the efforts of others in the organization. These connections and awareness levels are essential to individual achievement and greater overall team mission accomplishment.

Once your priorities are clearly set, time management becomes practically a mechanical task. The connections to other aspects of the flow of information and work in the organization bring valuable perspectives to life. Now time management can be a more meaningful skill, integrally related to the highly conscious conduct of business.

Time Management

Time management does not stand alone as an influencer of productivity. Time management is closely associated with staffing, work assignments, communication, and the organization's functions. All of these elements must be considered together if we are to significantly improve the use of the time available to our team. Each factor influences how time will be valued and used.

Parkinson's Law teaches us that "work expands to fill the time available." This law raises four concerns for us to consider:

1. Do people know everything that is expected of them, or are they simply assigned one task at a time? Do they understand the flow of work and how their contributions fit in?

    If they don't know what they can do next, many workers will "milk" a job . . . taking more time than necessary to finish. Sometimes this delay is intentional; most often it is not. Your guidance may be needed. Instill a sense of pride in getting things done within agreed-upon time frames.

    Do people have to wait for further direction, instead of being able to direct themselves to other work to be done? If you micro-manage, continually looking over people's shoulders and insisting they come to you for their next assignment, you severely limit their productivity . . . and yours. Focus on results. Let others manage their own activities to accomplish the results. Help them understand how to evaluate their own performance in terms of the investment of time, as well as other resources.

2. Are too many people assigned to accomplish a particular job?

    Perhaps there isn't enough work to go around, "forcing" people to do less and wasting time in the process. Rather than simply assigning staffing hours to jobs to be done, ask your people (who probably understand the work better than you do) what they believe is needed. Look, with your team members, for alternative uses of productive time once assigned jobs are completed. Ask for ideas on how more work can be accomplished by the team.

Inappropriate staffing can encourage misuse of time, and even send a message to workers that effective time management really is not that important. "Goofing off" can become accepted behavior. Many of the inappropriate staffing problems have been addressed in the downsizing campaigns waged by so many companies in recent years. This practice will not—and should not—stop. Leaders should be forever vigilant to prevent over-staffing—empire building, while assuring that sufficient resources are allocated to avoid undue stress. Stress causes people to make errors, forcing work to be re-done in a costly, unnecessary expenditure of time.

3. Are some of the assigned tasks just "busy work" to keep people occupied?

Not only is this busy work a flagrant waste of valuable time, it reinforces the feeling that productive use of time is not valued in the organization. "Busy work" assignments can also lower the self-esteem of your employees. They sense when their work and time are of little importance.

4. Is there a system for checking people's work?

Are there procedures for you, or someone else in a management or inspection capacity, to monitor work quality in a timely manner so people completing one job can move directly to another assignment? Or do some of your subordinates have to wait for approval before continuing? What mechanisms do you have for expediting your approvals to minimize time loss?

Many leaders, perhaps including you, spend a great

deal of time "treading water." There is a lot of activity, a lot of splashing around, but people are not making any progress. Usually, such leaders need to become more organized, with tighter focus on just what it is they are trying to accomplish.

Putting things in perspective, recognize that time is one of your greatest resources. Given time, you can do just about anything. Paradoxically, while you may never seem to have enough time, you have all that there is. This resource cannot be expanded, but you can strengthen your use of it by tapping into the time resources of your fellow workers. Challenge work allocation on a regular basis to assure the best return on your investment of time.

Management Techniques

Time is not your enemy. Time actually becomes your friend as you begin to plan and organize its use. With this shift in perspective, a reasonable amount of time spent planning and organizing is not wasted, but well-used. Intentionally set aside some time to think, to contemplate; that's considered to be one of the primary responsibilities of a good leader. Consider carefully, among all the activities that demand your time, which are the most important or most urgent. The most urgent are not necessarily the most important!

Writing some things down really helps. You cannot do what you cannot remember. Carry a pad or 3" x 5" cards with you. When something occurs to you, write it down. If you use a time planner, and I encourage you to do so, write all these notes in your planner. Keep everything in one place, and you'll avoid losing important ideas, reminders, and solutions. Instead of trying to do everything at once, laser-focus your effort on solving specific problems. You'll be delighted with your increased solution rate. Watch your efficiency climb!

Get yourself organized, within yourself and in your work environment. The better organized you are, the more effective you will be. Have you looked at your personal work space? Is it well-organized or not? The appearance of your office says a lot about you. Both you and your visitors receive clear messages about how well you have your "act" together. Contrary to the popular axiom, a messy desk is not the sign of an organized mind!

Organized leaders have a place for everything and keep things in their places. This organization enables you to function at a much higher level. Is your office littered with the paperwork flow that is part of your job? If so, you may be decreasing your effectiveness and creating a negative image among your co-workers.

If you want your team members to be well organized, you have to set the example. It's worth the investment in your time and in organization tools to send a strong message to others that you are in control of your work environment.

Your first move must be to establish a comfortable, simple system of organization. One highly effective tool for paperwork management is a tickler file. Using 43 ordinary file folders, label 12 of them with the months of the year. Label the other 31 numerically, representing the days of the month. Whenever you have a paper that will need attention at some future date, put it in the appropriate folder in your tickler file. Don't let unneeded papers accumulate on your desk.

For papers you're working on right now, create a priority system. Using file folders, in-baskets, or just designated places on your desk, sort papers by degree of importance. Those that need immediate attention could be labeled "Priority A." "Priority B" papers could be those of somewhat less importance. Routine papers could be sorted as "Priority C." "Priority D" could stand for "delegate" or "dump."

Don't have a actual "Priority D" pile, just make good use of your wastebasket and your "out" box. Throw out whatever papers you don't need. When delegating, get the papers off your desk onto someone else's. Remove the clutter to give yourself a stronger sense of organization and a clean workspace. Remember: "the wastebasket is your friend."

If the nature of your work requires you to have some quiet time to work on projects, write reports, or just think, set aside specific time in your schedule. During those hours, you simply are not available unless there is an emergency. Uninterrupted privacy is a powerful tool in maximizing the use of your time.

Physically close the door to your office, if you have one. If you don't have a door or a secure area, put a sign on the entrance to your cubicle or string a few strands of yarn across the doorway to psychologically block the entrance. While doing some work in England a few years ago, I learned another clever technique for signaling that you want to be left alone for a while. In this company, each employee had a stuffed animal mascot that served as a protector. When privacy was requested, the stuffed animal would be in plain view—on the desk or even blocking the doorway.

Be sure to create a system whereby people can leave you messages when you are not available. Post a notice (maybe in voicemail, too) announcing when you will again be available for conversations, consultations, or whatever.

If you cannot get that privacy in your office, find some secluded place like an empty office or a conference room where you can work undisturbed. Be careful, however, that you don't give your subordinates the impression that you are not accessible as their leader. Always let people know when you will be available again, whether that duration is 20 minutes or two hours.

A number of organizations, realizing that their leaders require "quiet time", have established periods during the day when managers don't interrupt each other unless it is critically important. Telephone calls are held for response at another time. It is amazing how much more these people can get accomplished without interruption. With staff support and a clear policy, all managers can be in "quiet time" mode at the same time—just like they were in conference together.

Another technique that many leaders have found valuable is to establish both starting and stopping times for their meetings, conferences, and interviews. Start meetings on time so people will know you are dependable and firm. Set a consistent standard. Respect those who are on time for the meeting by starting promptly. When there is an agreed-upon ending time, all parties concerned consciously move to get their business done quickly.

Written agendas, including questions to be answered or decisions to be made, make meetings more productive. This idea is particularly effective when the agendas are distributed to participants prior to the meetings. Show responsibilities for particular parts of the meeting, by name, so people can prepare appropriately. Specify what results are expected from the meeting.

Some organizations hold stand-up meetings. There are no chairs in the meeting room. Furnishings may consist of one or more tables, corkboard and/or erasable walls, and similar props for group communication. It is amazing how much more quickly meetings progress when all participants are standing!

You can learn more techniques for effective time management from the many books available in libraries and bookstores. Our purpose with this chapter has been to recognize the importance of the management of priorities and time in excelling organizations.

As a leader, you must intensely concentrate on your priorities. From that foundation, the management of your time becomes a matter of mechanically applying proven techniques. Remember, you are responsible for the priorities and time of your team members, as well as your own.

Emphasize to your people that time is a non-renewable resource. Everyone has to work together to make the best use of the time available to the team. A commitment to be sensitive to the use of time throughout the organization can have a significant, positive impact.

Thought-Provoking Questions

1. To what extent do you and your people legitimately manage your own time? Is this level of time management appropriate?
2. How well do your people understand your priorities? Why is this understanding important?
3. How do you measure your time management effectiveness? How can your results be improved?

Reader's Notes

Effective
Communications

A vital aspect of the excelling environment is that people within the organization communicate freely, openly, and effectively. They communicate well with peers, with superiors, and with subordinates. There are no obstacles to communications across departmental and functional lines within the organization. People take pride in the effectiveness of their communications with customers, suppliers, and others external to the organization. Thorough, pro-active communication is a conscious and deliberate process.

In the excelling environment, communication is interactive. That is, communication is a two-way rather than a one-way process. People talk with each other, rather than at each other. Managers encourage their team members to share with them information, opinions, ideas, and concerns. Questions are most welcome, especially when they will clarify job expectations or improve job performance.

As an excelling manager, you should definitely practice an open-door policy. Be receptive to anything your people want to share with you. However, be careful you don't fall into the "open-door trap." The open door policy means more than merely encouraging people to come to your office to talk about their concerns. Some people won't feel comfortable coming to your office. They may be intimidated because of your position or the location of your office. It's just not comfortable for them.

To overcome this perceived obstacle to open communications, spend a significant part of your time with your people in their work environment. Carry your open door with you! Invite, and be receptive to, whatever input you may receive from your people on their turf. If you're accessible to them, where it's comfortable for them to talk, they'll communicate more openly with you.

Get Closer to People

Give people the opportunity to communicate with you by getting close to them physically and psychologically. You can't interact with your people by staying in your office. You have to get up, get out, and get connected. This process starts with your immediate work group—the people who are closest to you, the people you interact with on a regular basis. Meet your people at their work stations, in the lunch/break room, or wherever else may be appropriate.

Initiate conversations with your people, asking questions that can't be answered with a yes or no response. Get them talking, while you listen and respond. With that experience, and their appreciation that you really do want to understand what's happening for them, other people will be much more likely to listen while you talk.

Getting close doesn't mean you have to snuggle up to each of your subordinates while they're working. A comfortable social distance is more appropriate, particularly in these times of sensitivity to sexual harassment.

A reasonable physical proximity is not at all difficult to achieve. We're talking about you deliberately being available, reachable, responsive. You'd be surprised how many managers don't really make any concerted effort to be accessible to their people on a continual basis. If you close yourself off from your people, they lose their motivation to develop a better relationship with you.

Psychological closeness refers to your behavior. Sometimes the way you act overrides what you say. If you say you're eager to communicate with your people, for example, but are never around to talk with them, your actions will speak louder than your words. Others have to perceive from your behavior that you really are interested and that you're sincere about communicating openly, or they'll assume you're merely giving "lip service" to the concept of true communication.

What you say and how you say things are both important. Tell people what's going on. Give them information that will be of interest to them without their having to ask for it.

Many employees aren't even sure what questions to ask, but they do want more knowledge about their company, their fields, their careers, strategic plans, and their leaders.

Don't talk down to your subordinates. See them as co-equal members of your team and communicate with them on that basis. People don't like to be patronized. Your communication with them must be sincere. If you aren't genuine in your interest as you interact with them, you'll be seen as phony. People won't pay much attention to anything you say. Adopt the philosophy of servant leadership.

Servant leadership: leading others by attending to their needs so they can attend to yours. Servant leadership: supporting others so they can accomplish their work. Servant leadership: being of service to others—physically, psychologically, philosophically. It's a model that works well for thousands of leaders. Moving from a directive manager to a servant leader is a big shift; make the journey in small steps and it can be done. Once you decide on your style of leadership, the rest of the work comes easier. Remember, however, that it will not be easy for others to accept a radically different style when they've grown accustomed to who you are (or have been for a long period of time). Enlist their help in making your transition; it will make the process easier for both of you.

Be Open and Genuine

Department managers in a manufacturing company I consulted with faced a challenging problem: they had to produce an unusual amount of their product to meet an unexpected customer deadline. They met with their production workers and explained the problem. The managers laid the facts on the table, plain and simple. No double-talk. No threats. No pressure. During the meeting, they asked everyone to pitch in to help meet the customer's requirements.

Honestly and plainly sharing the reality of the situation with a sincere request for help worked: not only did the employees work faster, they voluntarily worked overtime to meet the need. Result: the job was shipped early, the customer was delighted, and the manufacturer gained several new customers from referrals from the satisfied customer.

In addition to your team members, there are people external to your organization with whom you need to communicate closely. Strong external communication is important for your effectiveness and your reputation in your marketplace. It also helps you internally. When your people see your consistency and sincerity with outsiders as well as your employees, it reinforces your ethical position . . . your trustworthiness. This congruence will serve you well.

Of your external stakeholders, your customers are the most important. Sharing your information and ideas with them is almost as important as listening to what they have to say.

Be especially sensitive to their concerns, questions, inquiries, and suggestions. The same recommendation applies to your suppliers. These people have information and insights that will be valuable to you and your organization. If you don't communicate openly with them, you may be left in the dark.

From my experience as a consultant, I also heartily recommend involvement in trade associations—local, regional, and national (or international). The sharing of ideas and experiences can save you countless dollars and hours, while giving you and your people an opportunity to help others. You never know when those favors will come back to you.

Again, getting close means being available to talk with other people on their turf. To communicate with your customers, suppliers, colleagues, you have to go to them. Invest the time to reach out this way. The return will be bountiful.

If you're in a retail business, spend some time on the sales floor talking with customers. It's what Jack Trout and Al Reis call "going down to the front" in their book, *Marketing Warfare.* Don't hesitate to conduct short, informal customer satisfaction interviews with your customers. Ask what they like best and least about your store. How can you improve your product lines, merchandising, or service? You normally won't get this kind of information unless you ask for it.

In non-retail businesses, you can benefit by going to your customers to learn more about their needs and how you can fill them. You'd be amazed at how many customers of manufacturing or service companies rarely see anyone other than a sales representative from the companies that supply them. If you're not in a position that directly serves outside customers, arrange to join someone who is. You'll probably learn a few lessons that could help you do your job even better. The end result will be enhanced effectiveness in serving your customers.

Enlightened companies are now sending their managers to suppliers' places of business to learn more about how the supplier does business. With a strengthened relationship, your suppliers can do an even better job for you. You'll better understand their capabilities and their needs. To help them understand what you're trying to do, invite their people in to see your operation. Their outside perspectives could result in significant improvements.

Some companies train suppliers' employees in quality control methods and other skills to enable them to do a better job producing what the company buys from them. Cooperative relationships are beginning to replace the traditional protective semi-suspicious relationships that have existed between customers and suppliers for so long.

To strengthen quality of a product, a manufacturer recently assigned two engineers to actually work in the facilities of a subcontractor. Together with the subcontractor's people, they eliminated some frustrating and costly "bugs", cooperatively producing a better product for the end user.

Other companies have sent people out to train customers' employees how to best use their products and services. Some companies engage outside professionals to provide management training, technical training, or informative speeches for their customers or clients. The extra care and concern is sincerely appreciated by the receiving company, strengthening the bonds between the two organizations.

A number of my clients have invited me in to deliver speeches or seminars for their customers. While it's a nice way to say "thank you," the information sharing also made the customers stronger so they could remain profitable and effective in their businesses . . . staying in business so they could buy from my client. Don Vlcek talks more about building relationships with suppliers in his book, *The Domino Effect*. It's all part of the shift toward more conscious vertical partnering in the world of business.

Take the initiative to get closer to your people, your customers, and your suppliers. Seek ways to be of service. You'll discover that improved communication can make a substantial difference. Be open to new ideas and let those with whom you are communicating know of your receptivity. When trying to solve problems or make improvements, an objective perspective from another organization could generate valuable input.

Attend your trade association's conferences. Absorb as much knowledge, insight, and experience as you can. Take some of your people with you, so they can experience the learning, caring, and sharing first-hand. When you return, talk with the folks back home about what you learned. If you took some others with you, have them involved in the reporting process. Report to your employees as if you were reporting to a client or your own board of directors, with respect and seriousness.

Communications Techniques

If you want to excel in your communications with your people, here are some practical techniques to become more successful.

1. Say Hello.

Greet your employees at the start of each work day. With your greeting, indicate your genuine appreciation that they are there to help you accomplish your objectives. You can do this just by the inflection and tone of your voice; you don't have to actually say those words every day.

Sound simple? It is. But surprisingly few supervisors or managers do it. Some employees go for days without their superiors even saying "hello" or "good morning". Your people want you to recognize their presence, their value. They want your respect, just as you want theirs.

2. Pass By.

As you walk through your workplace, you pass by your subordinates as they work. Be sure to say or do something positive to acknowledge every one of your subordinates every day. If you can talk with each person, just briefly, several times a day, that's even better.

Make your encounters with your people positive by noting something good about their performance, their work area, their appearance, or even just the weather. People are inspired more by upbeat comments than by negative or neutral expressions.

As you practice this technique, you'll be building more solid relationships with your people. You'll be giving them opportunities to talk with you. Be receptive, even to those who just seem to talk without really having anything significant to say at that moment. By giving people a little attention, you will be showing that you care.

3. Listen.

Our schools teach reading, writing, and speaking. Very few schools offer courses on listening, yet listening is probably the most important communications skill. Few people really know how to listen. There's a reason we have two ears and only one mouth. We should listen twice as much as we talk!

Actually, to be really effective, you should listen with more than just your ears. Listen with your eyes—look at people who are talking with you. Listen with your face and your body. Orient yourself toward those who are trying to send you messages. Sure, you can listen while doing something else or looking in another direction. But, do you really hear what is being said? And, just as vital, does the speaker feel your attention is focused on his/her message or somewhere else?

You can employ a technique known as "active listening". As you listen to someone, hear as much as you can of what is being communicated. Then paraphrase the message back to assure that you've heard correctly. Notice that you are assuming responsibility, in part, for the communication process. You're not placing the entire load on the speaker.

The other person will appreciate your obvious interest in what is being said. This feeling in itself will enhance the communication process.

Listening is one of the most important things you can do as an excelling manager. The importance of listening can't be emphasized enough. If you are open to genuine two-way communication, the people you work with will feel that you care about them. That feeling will be returned. This empathy will help strengthen your team, and thereby, your productivity.

4. Manage Meetings.

Most managers "hold" meetings. Excelling leaders manage them. Here are some things to consider:

Don't call meetings unless you have to. An increasing number of people in organizations, particularly in the management and staff ranks, complain that there are too many meetings. Respond to these concerns by making all your meetings productive. People want to get things done. They don't want to be stalled in seemingly useless meetings that rob them of the time they need to get their work done!

Meetings should improve productivity, not hamper it. In too many organizations, meetings slow down progress rather than expedite it. Promote the philosophy that meetings are work sessions, not social events. You might want to actually schedule some social get-togethers—no work to be discussed, just to support human relationships among your people. A meal is a good venue for this activity, like a no-work lunch.

When you do schedule a meeting, specify a starting time and an ending time. Start on time, even if everyone is not present. You'll soon get a reputation for being dependable and firm. When you say the meeting will start at 2:00, start at 2:00. The same policy applies to the ending time—even if you haven't finished with the agenda. You may have to schedule another meeting later to finish the agenda. Respect other people's time, and they'll respect yours. You'll find your meetings becoming more results-oriented and productive.

Agendas serve several purposes. First, they tell partici-pants what will be covered during the meetings. Second, they help keep you organized as the meeting leader. Third,written agendas can prevent you from going off on tangents.

If decisions are to be made at the meeting, state those ques-tions or issues on the agenda or meeting announcement. It's wise to send the agendas to participants prior to the meeting. People should have enough notice and information to prepare adequately for their effective participation in the meeting.

For many reasons, a clearly written set of minutes should be distributed to participants and other concerned individuals soon after the session. Specify decisions made, actions taken, responsibilities assigned, and follow-up needed. If possible, include an announcement about the time and place of the next meeting. These official minutes will help clarify the proceed-ings, minimizing ambiguity and eliminating confusion.

5. Take Notes

Another effective technique is to take notes on what other people are saying. This obvious activity demonstrates that you want to be sure you understand and remember what is being communicated to you. Use this method with discretion. Some people will appreciate your obvious interest; others will feel that your taking notes while they talk is rude. You may want to ask permission: "Do you mind if I take a few notes as we talk so I can better remember what we've discussed?"

Take notes in private meetings. Take notes in staff meet-ings. Keep the notes in file folders, your planner, or in a com-puter program like ACT!® Having a record to go back to in the future will be helpful, and when people see you taking notes they'll have less tendency to change or challenge con-tent or context at a later date.

Note: be careful that your note taking doesn't interfere with your eye contact and connection with others in the meetings. If you're too intensely focused on note taking, you may miss the "big picture" of what's happening.

6. Use Bulletin Boards.

Most organizations have employee bulletin boards. These can be used by you, as a manager, to communicate with your people. Things that people need to see, read, and refer to, can be posted on bulletin boards. How well are you utilizing this communications tool in your organization?

Extend your thinking beyond the traditional thumb-tack bulletin board. Technology now allows us to post items to electronic bulletin boards for internal and/or external consumption. You can even design your bulletin board so people who view your posting can click on a check-off box or send you a message to indicate that they have read the information you wanted them to see.

7. Memorandums.

Memos can be an effective means of sharing information with your people, but be careful not to overuse this medium of communication. Most organizations are trying to reduce unnecessary paperwork, a well-advised effort. Use memos when people need to have something in writing, when the subject matter applies specifically to a certain group of people. Written records are also important when people will need to have the information in their hands to follow-up on the matter discussed with some sort of action.

Use standard formats for memos to make them easier to read and absorb. Write clearly and concisely, emphasizing the main points. If people in your organization have difficulty doing this, some workshops on business writing may be needed.

One company's efficiency was hampered by an overwhelming mountain of hard-to-read memos. A writing consultant was engaged to train employees to write in a more organized fashion. People learned how to eliminate extra words and phrases, focusing on the specific message they wanted to communicate. Adopting a tighter writing style shortened the memos and made them much more effective.

Less time was invested in writing and reading them, leaving more time to accomplish the real work of the company.

Encourage people to discard memos after reading if they don't need to keep the information on file. Written communication is valuable for clarity, but that doesn't mean we have to file every memo we receive. Consider actually marking a memo, "discard after reading" or "no need to file." In our firm, we use a rubber stamp that reads "Read & Discard" that saves us all a lot of time . . . and filing cabinet space!

If your memo should be kept by the recipient, indicate where it should be filed. For example, "file in Personnel Policy Manual at the end of Section 4c." Being a little more thorough and specific in your communication often makes life easier for others.

8. Eliminate "FYI" notations.

How many times have you received a clipping or memo or something with a cryptic note reading "FYI," the abbreviation for "For Your Information"? In most cases, I imagine your first reaction was "who sent this . . . and why do they want me to read it?" Make it a policy in your organization to sign FYI notes. Ask that anyone sending an FYI to someone add an explanation of what you want the recipient to note . . . and why. Use a highlighter or otherwise mark pertinent sections or sentences you want others to see.

9. Employee Newsletters.

To share information with all your employees, a regularly published newsletter may be the answer. It doesn't have to be anything fancy, but it should be produced on a dependable, scheduled basis—not just sporadically. Regularity of publication will lend strength to this communications tool.

Newsletters should carry company information that may be of interest or value to employees. Personal items about employees (and their families) might be included. Some information about your industry, the marketplace, your customers or suppliers adds a valuable dimension in helping your employees better understand their company and their working environment.

Rather than just distributing the company newsletter in the workplace, consider mailing it your employees' homes. The publication will have a better chance of being read by each employee, instead of getting buried in other paperwork. Another benefit is that the newsletter will probably be read by your employees' families, as well as your employee. This added communications initiative could build family support for your employee's relationship with your organization.

Depending on how your newsletter is put together, it may also serve as a good public relations tool. A number of companies send copies of their in-house publications to their customers and suppliers. It's a nice way to share positive information about your organization with those who care about you and your people.

10. Be Creative.

Consider other ways you can enhance open communications among all the members of your team. Some other ideas that have been successful are company picnics, company "days" at amusement parks, pre-work continental breakfasts with food and beverages furnished by the employer, and educational programs offered after work for employees and their spouses.

Seek innovative ideas for building understanding. Your objective is to build more effective communication, resulting in closer, more meaningful relationships. Open communication among the members of your team will foster trust, job satisfaction, and higher productivity and that will result in building competence, confidence, and growth.

Thought-Provoking Questions

1. Many employees perceive their boss as having an open

door, but a closed mind. How can you counteract this perception?

2. Why should your people believe what you are communicating to them?

3. What can you do to assure that your communication is received as you are transmitting it?

Reader's Notes

15

Building Competence, Confidence, and Growth

When workers are confident about what they are doing, they do a better job. They are more satisfied with their work environment and are more internally motivated to excel. Worker confidence builds stronger productivity.

Confidence comes from a powerful combination of competence and experience. People feel stronger when they gain specific competencies to perform assigned tasks. Their achievements and capacities are reinforced by self-recognized high achievement, and positive input from superiors, co-workers, and customers. The experience portion comes from actually doing what they have prepared to do, so they can "feel" what it's like.

Sources of Competence

Each of your team members needs to feel competent to perform the tasks expected by you, by your organization, and by your customers. The building of that competence is a shared responsibility, shared between you and your subordinates.

Some competencies the employee brings along when hired to work for you. Other competencies are built while in your employ. Your responsibility as an excelling manager is to gain an understanding of existing competencies, and build from there on an individual basis with each employee. Rarely are a person's competencies fully described on a resume. You have to dig beneath the documentation of the obvious to discover the "real" person.

Competence to produce work of value includes the employee's talents, abilities, knowledge, and skills. Some of these competencies were gained in high school, trade school, college, or the armed forces. Others were developed through experience, both on and off the previous job(s). Some abilities "come naturally"—mechanical ability, for example. During formal leader-follower interviews, explore with each of your team members what abilities, knowledge, skills, and potential are included in that employee "package."

In a discussion with each employee, consider what competencies are needed now and in the future. Prepare a written list of those desired competencies for each member of your team. Listen to what competencies the employee would like to develop personally, in addition to those that the company desires. Check off those areas in which the employee is already competent.

Next, with your team member, carefully design a deliberate plan of individual professional development. Determine alternative methods for the employee to gain the competencies. Set priorities, select most appropriate growth alternatives, and develop a meaningful schedule for growth.

The growth and development of your employees should be shared between the employee and the employing organization. The employee should assume some specific responsibility for personal growth beyond what the employer provides. And, of course, the employee should invest full energies in gaining from employer-provided opportunities.

Many companies reimburse employees for costs of tuition, fees, and books incurred while taking courses as part of degree- or certificate-granting programs. As needed, some companies grant time off or adjust schedules to enable employees to take classes during normal working hours. Such support encourages people to continue their personal development and builds loyalty toward the supporting employer.

It is accepted today that employers are justified in covering the cost of training that is directly related to the employee's current or prospective position. Broader education that will enrich the employee may be paid for by the employer and/or the employee. Each employer sets his/her own guidelines as to how this matter will be handled. You should become familiar with your organization's policies. Enlightened companies will expand their definitions of training and education to provide for a wide range of learning experiences, on and off the job. Building stronger people pays wonderful dividends later on.

On-the-job training and work experience can help build competencies. Many organizations use senior employees to teach younger or less-experienced employees how to do their jobs. This is good thinking and a good use of talent, particularly if the company encourages collaboration, creative thinking, and vertical teaming. Jobs are changing so rapidly, however, that the "old dogs" may not be able to fathom, let alone teach, the "new tricks." As employees learn their jobs and become proficient at assigned duties, they seek ways to enrich their jobs by adding additional duties that are different and more challenging than the normal responsibilities of the position. Give people the freedom, and encouragement, to grow. Keep growing your supervisors, too, or before long the workers will know much more than their "elders" know or even understand.

Cross-training, accomplished through formal classes and/or on-the-job experiential training, is being done more and more as organizations tighten their belts and ask employees to expand their capabilities and work responsibilities. Even if they don't perform the work on a regular basis, your employees will expand their competencies as they learn how to do jobs different from their own.

You strengthen your team's capacity to produce, for example, if a member of the team is missing due to illness or some other reason. If each employee has the knowledge and skills to assume another's responsibilities in an emergency, everyone feels more confident as a result. They cannot only fill-in when needed, but can interchange jobs to break monotony or bolster needs to complete a particular job.

Some companies experience heavier workloads in different departments at different times of the day. Cross-training can maximize employee productivity by enabling companies to switch people from one department to another as work progresses through a shop on a daily basis. I'm reminded of the story of a small manufacturing plant that concentrated its resources on production during the day so everything could be shipped on the same day it was produced. Toward the end of the day, people from the beginning of the production process joined administrative staff people in the shipping department to get the finished products packed and out the door.

An increasing number of organizations (over 226,000 in the United States alone, according to *TRAINING Magazine*) offer formal learning opportunities sponsored by the employer. Using internal training staffs and/or external resources, these employers offer seminars, workshops, lectures, and courses to their people. Some are mandatory; some are voluntary. Find out what is offered by your organization and learn how to arrange for your team members to participate. If there is not already a strong training and development function in your organization, take the initiative and form a task force to put one together. Build an internal capacity to train others, or establish relationships with outside vendors.

An increasing number of employers are contracting with professional trainers to design and conduct workshops, seminars, and classes intended to accomplish specific personnel development objectives. If enough members of your organization need strengthening of certain competencies, this alternative might be the best approach for you. The yellow pages or the closest chapter of the American Society for Training and Development will be resources to find training consultants and specialists to invite in for interviews.

Many organizations send employees to educational programs offered by outside vendors for people from a number of organizations. Most active among these providers are community colleges, universities, and companies that specialize in marketing and presenting public seminars and workshops around the country.

Your human resources professionals and/or senior management will be able to help you arrange the best program for your people. Take a pro-active role in seeking internal and external growth opportunities for yourself and your people. Everybody wins.

Employees will be more likely to attend seminars, workshops, or courses if the company is paying the fee. However, they may have more commitment to learning if asked to pay part of the cost. A reimbursement of all costs upon successful completion of a course may be a wise win-win strategy. Employers are encouraged to pay for all job-related learning, and cover at least part of the cost of broader, applicable education. Establish a policy about how these opportunities and obligations are met in your organization, then be sure to send approved copies to every employee.

As appropriate, you should encourage your people to become involved in the activities of their trade or professional organizations. These groups meet regularly on a local basis, offering formal and informal learning opportunities as people from different employers share ideas, experiences, and approaches to getting things done.

These industry groups offer an added benefit in the educational programs and exposure provided at state, regional, and national meetings. Whenever possible, enable your people to participate in these conferences and conventions. Be alert to special educational opportunities offered by such groups. Explore opportunities for volunteers from your organization to become involved in learning and practice, and assign responsibilities to others.

Another, somewhat exciting, way that competency can be built is to allow people to experiment with new ideas and methods. Remember that many of your people have great ideas to improve the way things are done; they're closest to the work and can often see things that managers and engineers can't. Allow them to work, independently or together, on innovative approaches. They and the company could benefit from the learning experience as well as the potential results. The limiting philosophy of "we've always done it that way" can be overcome!

Enthusiastically Share Knowledge

Another way to build the confidence of your people is to help them learn and understand more about your organization. The more open management is about sharing relevant information, the more knowledgeable the employees will be. And, equipped with this knowledge and trust, the more dedicated and loyal the employees will be. This knowledge, and the partnership engendered by sharing, will foster a sense of belonging and personal responsibility to help achieve desired results.

Knowledge about what's happening in the organization could have direct or indirect bearing on performance, depending on how related the knowledge is to the actual accomplishment of the person's duties. With more knowledge, invaluable relationships are built and workers gain insights to make better decisions about in-company transfers that make sense for them. In any case, they will know more about where you're trying to go and how you're going to get there. It's a lot easier to inspire people to high performance and loyalty when they understand the big picture.

There are a number of categories of information that would be interesting to your employees. You may have answers to these questions . . . or, you may not. Without these answers, your people are less likely to have the broad visionary knowledge of where you're going, why and when. As they collect pieces of this puzzle, they build a commitment to the employer, the field, themselves, and the function of the enterprise they are expected to support. They begin to understand what's happening and why, and they discover the vital role they can play. Share information that answers questions like

- What products and/or service does your organization produce? How well?
- What marketplace does your organization operate in? Why? How well?
- What's the competition like? How do you compare to your principal competitors?
- What do your productivity measurements look like? Why are they important?
- Facts and figures about sales volume, trends in the field, and how the company is doing on the stock market are all of interest to your people.

Whenever you present facts and figures, also provide a means for understanding how to read and interpret them. Answer those "why" questions. Your employees hear about management's decisions, but rarely about how the decisions are actually made. This deeper comprehension will be appreciated by your people, and will serve to guide their short- and long-term decision making.

Knowledge you want to share can be communicated through newsletters, memos, or employee meetings. Such a meeting might be held for all employees, or you might want to have divisional or departmental meetings. Factors about holding meetings depend on the size, structure, and geographic dispersal of your people.

The most effective way to communicate important pieces of timely information is to carefully pass the knowledge down through the levels of management. You can use formal meetings or just informal passage through supervisors to front-line employees.

If any information is going to be released to the general public through the news media, be sure your employees learn about it in a timely manner. No one wants to learn significant information about his/her organization from the news media. Keeping employees in the dark is decidedly counter-productive to building a sense of belonging and mutual trust. Establish a means whereby employees can read your company's press releases before they are released.

Mentoring

Another method for fostering personal and professional growth is the mentoring process. While the concept is relatively new to the work environment, historical tales offer numerous examples dating back to the days of Homer, the Greek poet. Informal mentoring has been strengthening people and organizations for many years, but an increasing number of companies are formalizing the process as part of their training and development program.

A formalized program will certainly work in a number of organizations, but informal mentoring will continue to have a strong impact. A structured system is not necessary for mentoring to be successful. Some mentors and their protégés will spend a lot of time together; others will have more occasional relationships. Some mentor/protégé relationships will be of relatively short duration; others will endure for very long periods of time.

"Mentor" means teacher. A mentor is a person who helps another learn and grow. Sometimes mentors are the direct supervisors of their protégés, quite often they are not. Sometimes the relationship is well-known; sometimes it is very private. While each relationship is different, the purpose is the same. The mentor, a more experienced or learned member of the team, helps a less competent/confident member grow and develop.

A mentoring relationship is usually initiated by the protégé. Desiring to grow and enhance his/her position within the organization, he/she seeks out one or more mentors to help guide that growth and development. The mentor could be a superior, a more senior person in another part of the organization, or a co-worker with more experience or knowledge.

Mentor/protégé relationships may also be initiated by someone who seeks to help a potential star performer. In this case, the subordinate may be flattered by the attention, faith, and potential, but both parties must be willing to enter into the relationship. They must be dedicated and committed to the mentorship or it won't work.

You may want to encourage this kind of relationship among your people. You may want to serve as a mentor to others in your organization, and you may reap considerable benefit by seeking mentors of your own. As the participants in these relationships help each other, the individuals and the organization strengthen the excelling potential.

Mentors help their protégés learn how to solve problems, how to think critically, and how to perform more professionally. They give advice, share what they've learned, and give encouragement. It's a motivating friendship with mutual benefits.

As an excelling leader, you have a professional obligation to help others grow. It's like lighting another's candle from your own flame. Your flame is not diminished by giving energy to another. The stronger light that results will build a better future for all concerned.

The End Result

Developing employee competence, sharing knowledge about the organization, and mentoring all build confidence. A positive result is a higher level of self-esteem on the part of all involved employees. These employees are more dedicated and productive, more likely to want to excel at whatever they do for their employer. The end result is a strong sense of commitment to the organization, the group goals, and to personal growth and development.

Thought-Provoking Questions

1. How can you build the competence of your people?
2. Explain the connection between competence and confidence. Apply this insight to your own work situation.
3. How might the concept of mentoring apply to you as a person and as a manager?

Reader's Notes

16

Commitment

The traditional management approach is to apply the basic tenets of the management cycle: planning, organizing, leading, and controlling. Many managers have been trained to place the emphasis on controlling. "Get the people going on what has to be done, then watch everything like a hawk."

As taught in management courses at colleges and universities, there are three aspects, or steps, to the controlling process:

1. Measure the performance;
2. Compare the actual performance against the objective (expectations); and
3. Make any adjustments necessary to bring performance into compliance with plans as necessary, change the plans to make them more realistic or legitimate.

Responsibility for control is placed squarely on the shoulders of the manager under this "traditional" style of

management. To a large degree, accountability for performance rests there also, since the worker is functioning as a
sort of tool of management to achieve results.

In an increasing number of organizations, we have shift-
ed away from this role of management. The trend now is for
employees to gradually assume individual responsibility for
the portion of the organization's work assigned to them. The
employees are expected to perform their tasks without management looking over their shoulders all the time. The age of
personal accountability has arrived. More and more employees will be seeking this higher level of accountability, though
many managers will find it difficult to let go of their controlling power.

Under this philosophy of personal accountability, each
employee is dedicated to completing assigned responsibilities correctly and on-schedule. The front-line employee is
gaining a greater voice in determining what those responsibilities will be. We expect employees to be committed to
what they are doing for their employer, and many employees
are so committed based on their own values and perspectives
on their organizational roles.

Need for Leadership

All this rhetoric sounds good, but employees can't run
the entire operation without leadership. The manager is still
an important part of the system. What we are finding, however, is that the manager's role is changing. No longer is the
manager expected to be directly in control of everything.
Instead, that aspect of the operation is now shared with other
members of the manager's work group. The sharing of the
managerial load relieves the manager to provide other kinds
of support—to make it easier for people to do their jobs in an
outstanding way.

As workers become more committed to high achievement in the workplace—doing things right, the first time, on

time—the need for control does not evaporate. It's still there, but as more of a process rather than a specific management responsibility. The same concerns of measurement, comparison, and correction still exist, but they're being addressed by people closer to the action of the organization.

Non-managerial employees are expected to measure their own production against the pre-established expectations. If correction is needed, the employee either handles it personally, if it is within his/her control, or refers the problem to the manager and/or peers for follow-up and resolution.

The manager's role is one of overseeing the entire operation, monitoring overall performance, and providing support to the employees who are producing the products or services of the organization. Companies are modifying their control mechanisms to accommodate this new approach. Rules and procedures are changing, usually for the better, and sometimes to the chagrin of the more traditional employees who seek to avoid any kind of change. Most of today's employees embrace these shifts, wanting to play a larger, more identifiable role in the accomplishment of goals.

With these changes, we're seeing some new concepts introduced to the production functions of our organizations. The concepts are Ethics and Integrity. All employees are expected to be ethical in their dealings and in their control of quality. Whatever they send out the door to the customer has to be right. The morality of decisions made has taken on new importance.

Integrity and Other Values

Integrity has become a vital part of the corporate scene, placing new obligations and pressures on all those working for our organizations. These issues haven't really been raised that strongly or obviously before. Now they have become an integral thread of our national industrial fabric. Given some recent shifts in cultural attitudes in our society, employers will emphasize integrity issues even more in the future.

Corporate integrity begins with personal integrity, as expressed and demonstrated by the organization's leaders. The practice of high integrity will often be obvious, accepted, even taken for granted. That "of course that's what we do" performance is laudable and should be encouraged. But we can go further. We can talk about integrity, bring it right up to the surface. Explain to people—your employees, customers, and suppliers when you make clear, significant, and perhaps position-setting decisions based on integrity issues. Expose the fact that the foundation for the decision was an application of your corporate integrity.

Others will understand, will support, and will bask proudly in the spotlight you'll shine on "doing things the right way."

Moral values are now a conscious aspect of organizational life, even to the extent that some companies are including references to "Christian principles" in their mission statements. In my consulting work, helping corporate leaders design their mission statements, I have comfortably accepted such orientations . . . as long as the leaders clarify—and articulate—a clear and concise idea of what "Christian principles" or any other descriptive phrase should really mean to those who read it and work with it.

Interpretation of such values is imperative, whether we call them Christian principles or something else. Reaching from the top of the organization down to the newest employee, the understanding and commitment must be consistent and real. Assure clear articulation of these values, with translation into how the values are applied in your work. What do these values mean in terms of productivity, quality, and customer service orientation? There must be clear understanding, even to the point of explaining values and their meaning during job interviews so applicants know concisely what will be expected of them.

One of my clients integrated their concepts of "Christian

Principles" thoroughly into their mission statement and their statement of guiding principles. They use their corporate statements continually—in the hiring process. Applicants are shown the statements before they are given applications to complete. They're asked to consider carefully how comfortable they are in committing to the statements and what they represent. If they're not comfortable with any aspect of what they see, they should not bother filling out the application; they won't be happy and neither will be the employer. At last reckoning, one-third of the applicants declined to complete the application!!

Note: there is a dangerous tendency to concentrate efforts on enculturating new employees. Don't forget the current members of your workforce. Be sure they're on-board with your philosophies, your values, your principles. Otherwise, you run the risk of having newer employees negatively influenced (or at least non-supported) in their corporate beliefs.

Making Things Happen

The anticipation that high quality products will be consistently produced is becoming more commonplace. Managers are learning a new philosophy: "expect more, and you'll get it." And, much to the surprise of some "old line" managers, that philosophy is working! People want to be significant and productive members of their work organization; they'll work hard to achieve and maintain that involvement.

As we discussed in Chapter 7, a vital part of the leader's job is to help set goals, give their people what they need to get the job done, and then get out of their way to let them do it. People can accomplish wonderful things without someone sitting on their shoulder.

We don't need to control so heavily anymore. We don't need to be out in the work area "cracking the whip." As employees perceive their roles, understand their expectations, and receive support, their commitment to their work is increasing. We can expect to see more of this happening in American organizations, with less of the heavy-handed control autocratic management style which has been so prevalent.

Major stumbling blocks in this change process may be managers themselves. If they've received any management training, the message has often been, "you're in charge; you're in control." The changing management styles, such as we've postulated in this book, are perceived as a threat by many managers, particularly those who have been around for quite a while and have had the old style ingrained so deeply that it's difficult to change.

With the shift to the personal commitment style, you won't have less control. You'll just have a different kind of control. There's no question that this shift is a dramatic break from tradition, but this new way of doing things is gaining increasing acceptance across the country and in a range of different fields and industries.

Members of the organization, from top to bottom and in every department or function, commit to doing their absolute best. Each employee is internally motivated to perform at maximum potential, regardless of what the task may be. Following the role model of dedicated leadership, everyone adopts the commitment to doing what needs to be done to excel.

This approach may sound rather idealistic to some readers. Yes, we recognize that it won't work with every single employee. There will still be those workers who have been brought up with such strong negative attitudes about work organizations that they will resist your efforts. Some of these people learned those attitudes and behaviors in their work environment. As long as your environment reflects those attitudes, you won't be able grow and change yourself. They will gradually change when they feel they can trust you and what you say.

Your credibility will be established as these people discover for themselves that they can believe you, that you will back up your words with consistent action. It takes time. Don't expect overnight miracles. That kind of rapid response isn't likely to occur. Be patient and persistent. Strive to build trust and mutual commitment in small steps.

One of three things will happen:

1. People will accept your approach and become supportive and committed;
2. They will build an increasing discomfort working in an environment where they are not part of the mainstream and leave on their own; or
3. They will provide you with opportunities to initiate disciplinary action eventually removing them from your workforce.

Commitment is essential for organizations to thrive in today's world. Those who cannot feel that sense of commitment should move to another work environment where they can feel it. Increasingly, people at all levels are recognizing this fact and making career change decisions for themselves. This recognition places a new and important burden on you to help build the kind of environment that will attract and hold the kind of people you want to work with you.

Commitment requires self-discipline. You must focus on your values and your goals, striving to keep your behavior consistent with those critical elements. While your work is serious, find pleasure in what you are doing. As has been said by many, "take your work seriously, but don't take yourself too seriously." If you don't enjoy your work, you probably should seek something else to do with your time and your life.

Your joy for life should manifest itself in your obvious enthusiasm for all your activities. This positive feeling should be found in your work, family relationships, social activities, and your private time.

When you demonstrate this feeling of enthusiasm, you'll discover it's contagious! Those around you, in all environments, will respond to your attitude with similar behaviors.

Conversely, if you exhibit a negative attitude, you can expect that to be adopted just as readily.

Along with this self-disciplined commitment comes a need for both balance and consistency in your life. Keep your life activities in perspective. Look objectively at what you are doing. Take time to think. Avoid helter-skelter, crisis-oriented management by investing time to contemplate what you are doing and why you are doing those things. Keep a clear head, with your feet firmly grounded in reality.

An increasing number of organizations are operating with a philosophy of conscious commitment to values, mission, and goals. Top quality professionals entering the job market, the kind of people your organization probably wants to hire, are seeking companies with a modern, enlightened management style. Will your organization be able to respond to these changing values and approaches?

Now is the time to examine your commitment, from the most senior to the newest employee. Commitment is more than just words on paper. It's a part of your mission. It's a part of the way you do business. It's real. It's you.

Thought-Provoking Questions

1. What does "integrity" mean to you? How can you demonstrate this vital concept to your people?
2. It may be difficult for some managers to shift from a directive/controlling style to a support/commitment style. How can you help them make the change comfortably?
3. How will you respond to employees who refuse to commit to cooperative participation on your work team?

Reader's Notes

17

Internal Motivation/Desire

Excelling can occur, on a personal and organizational basis. It probably won't be easy, given all the forces pushing against it. Even if you're the only one in your organization striving to excel, you can still make a difference. Obviously, the more people who dedicate themselves to excelling, the greater chance you have to be a leading organization in your field and in your community. Your work will be easier as you recruit others to join your crusade for excelling performance.

There's no sense kidding ourselves. It takes work. Excelling is the hard way, not the easy way. It's a lot easier to just let the organization atrophy by not continually encouraging excelling. Just as muscles lose their strength if not stretched and exercised, the natural process is for the system to weaken. We all know that maintaining a diligent program of physical exercise is a challenge. It takes perseverance, concentration, investment of time, and certainly and expenditure of energy. Excelling in all activities demands similar dedication.

Moving toward excelling gets easier as progress is made, but that takes time. To make excelling work, you must be committed and patient. The increased performance and achievement will gradually come. As that glorious period comes to life, your sense of satisfaction and pride will defy description!

The first step is simple: you must want to excel, and you must want to help your people excel. You can't just say, "I suppose it's a good idea." You must have a burning desire to make it work. The oft-cited "fire in the belly" must be hot! A high level of enthusiasm makes a tremendous difference. You'll probably have to make some significant changes in the way you manage, in the way you lead. But you'll be growing. With both change and growth comes pain—the pain of frustration, disappointment, and the discomfort of recognizing your own shortcomings and having to overcome those "deficiencies". Expect short-term pain, but long-term gain.

Excelling is not something that only *other* people do. *You* must personally accept the challenge. Not everyone will be able to do it. If it were easy, more people would be practicing the principles of excelling and there would be no need for this book. You may even encounter complicated situations that you'll have to deal with on your own, or perhaps with some help from mentors or members of your support group.

Remember that excelling is a process. Your journey to higher achievement will begin as you put into practice the ideas and techniques presented in this book. You'll begin slowly and move forward step-by-step. Your journey will never end. Excellence is not a result, it's a lifestyle. It's a vital philosophy that will influence everything you do.

Overcoming the Fear

Effectively practicing *The Process of Excelling* will be very difficult for many managers. The excelling approach requires you to work with your people in a different way than you may have ever before experienced. You'll give up some of the control that so many managers crave, cherish, and guard jealously. You won't be "in command" in the same sense anymore. Results will be greater, stress will be lower, fulfillment will be higher; but these benefits will come for different reasons.

Strength as a manager comes in different forms. You don't have to exercise tight control over people's lives to have strength and influence. Potency, power, and effectiveness as a manager comes from your leadership style and how well you support your people to achieve desired results. Productivity doesn't come from forcing people to do things. True high productivity comes from people producing at their best possible level of quality and quantity because they *want* to.

That "want to" is generated by how you perform as a leader. As you become more comfortable with the excelling style of management and leadership, you'll inspire an increasing desire on the part of your team members to excel along with you. When you desire to do your best and draw the best from others, it shows in your behavior; you'll see the changes start to happen. Don't expect overnight miracles; they won't happen. That's why we call this a process, not a quick fix.

There is, however, a strong potential of seeing some indication of results relatively soon. It comes because people are hungry for the kind of leadership we've encouraged in this book. They want it and will respond to it . . . if and when they believe it's real. Expect it. Look for it. As you observe it, you will be inspired personally by the feedback to continue to move toward higher achievement for yourself and for your work group.

Along with the fear of letting go, of moving away from tight control in the managerial sense, you may also experience both fear of failure and fear of success. Each of these fears is very real and will affect your performance if you don't face them and deal with them. These feelings are normal, so don't think there's something wrong with you if the change, the shift, is uncomfortable at first.

Your fear of failure may be fed by the fact that much of what is proposed in this book may be new to you. Some managers and their organizations have been doing some of these things for years. For others, excelling leadership will be a brand new concept. Different. Scary. Excelling leadership will seem risky.

Sure, there is the possibility that you will fail in your attempts to excel, but only if we're talking about failure being the lack of achieving everything you'd like to accomplish. Recognize that even a few tentative steps along the path of excelling will be progress. Each thing you do will be an improvement, and each improvement—no matter how small—is a foundation for further growth.

You may think it's silly to talk about fear of success, but that fear is very real for a number of people. Much of this fear comes from uncertainty about what success will look and feel like. How will you deal with it? Will it be just a flash in the pan, or will you be able to achieve some permanency with your success? How might your superiors respond to your increased capacity and results? How might your life be different?

You can overcome this fear through a technique called "visualization." Visualize the situation you are trying to achieve. How does it look? How does it feel? How do you feel? How do others around you feel? As you become comfortable with the image of where you want to be, it will be much easier to go there. You'll be more prepared to cope with this exciting new experience.

Why Bother?

With the recognition that excelling won't be easy, that applying the principles presented in this book will be challenging and difficult, you may ask, "why bother?". That's a legitimate question that you must answer for yourself before you can proceed. This decision is really a matter of personal choice for you.

Some people will decide that it's not worth the effort. They'll simply continue doing business as usual. And, for some of them, that will work satisfactorily for what they—and others—expect. For others, the negative decision will block many employees from achieving their best performance. Eventually, this reluctance to excel in leadership and achievement will damage careers that are not developing and ruin businesses that can no longer compete.

Our marketplace will demand more and more high quality in both merchandise and services. Excelling quality. Customers—businesses and end consumers—will consciously seek higher levels of performance from people and organizations they deal with. This expectation will naturally flow over into how we lead our people and manage our organizations. Our people, our stakeholders will have increasingly higher expectations about what happens in the work organization environment.

If you do decide to begin practicing the principles of *The Process of Excelling*, your work will gradually become easier. The people you lead will be more supportive, more committed to their work. As your leadership emphasizes planning, and this effort filters down through the levels of the organization, each employee will gain a clearer understanding of what is expected. You will then have a much better chance of achieving those expectations.

As people consciously work more in concert, stress levels, at least negative stress, will be reduced. Work groups will become teams, and each member will assume personal responsibility and accountability for the team work to be done.

As this attitude, behavior, and achievement spread through your organization, you'll start making a more powerful impact on the marketplace. Your organization's competitive position will improve, enhancing job security for you and your people. Customers will perceive you as delivering more value and will strengthen their bonds of loyalty toward you.

As the sense of excelling takes hold, your employees will develop a sincere and influential feeling of pride. This feeling will be evident in the workplace and in your community. Your quality reputation will spread. As a result, when you seek new employees, you'll discover more applicants of higher caliber indicating their desire to work with you. Customers and suppliers will have different feelings toward you . . . a new respect.

The overall image of your organization will be positively affected—in your industry, your community, and your marketplace. More and more people will want to do business with you, strengthening your entire business stature. People naturally want to be associated with excelling organizations, and that includes yours.

Practice excelling and you'll feel a change in yourself. Your self-image will improve and you'll realize significantly more satisfaction from your job. The excelling expectations and behaviors will flow over into your personal attitude and behavior, affecting the relationships between you and significant other people in your life.

Does it all sound idealistic? Like a dream? Perhaps. But executives, leaders, managers, and organizations that have applied only parts of what we have defined as *The Process of Excelling* have discovered the kind of results we're suggesting are possible. It's not difficult, and it's not brain surgery. It's common sense, applied through the heart.

The journey begins with a single step . . . your step.

Begin your journey.

Thought-Provoking Questions

1. How do you feel about what you've read so far in this book? Does it make sense for you? How can you apply the principles of *The Process of Excelling* in *your* organization?
2. What results can you expect from practicing excelling behaviors in your workplace?
3. How much can you do alone? Why do you need other people? What might you do to get them involved?
4. Can you use the visualization technique in a group setting? Try it.

Reader's Notes

Building the Feeling/Energizing

To implement the high performance excelling behaviors in your organization, begin by building on your existing foundation. You *already* have a lot of assets to apply:

1. One of the most important of these assets is *you*. There is vital power in your understanding of the excelling process, and your strong desire to make it work. Your dedication, commitment, and energy are essential for positive results.

    If you don't sincerely believe in the concept of excelling, it won't happen. You must be personally involved, *invested*. Your leadership will make the difference. If it isn't genuine, others will sense your skepticism and they won't follow you. In fact, they may even ridicule your phony leadership.

2. Another asset is your fellow managers. As they appreciate what you want to do, and enlist to join you in making positive changes, you will create a powerful synergy.

    As they lend their support, your combined energy reaches beyond what any one of you could possibly do alone. The key is for everyone to be singing from the same sheet of music. Powerful horses can exert strength to pull heavy loads; when they're harnessed so they're working together, their combined strength is much more effective than if they were each pulling in separate directions.

3. Your third asset is the fine people who currently work for your organization. Excelling is to their benefit, too. Deep down inside they want to excel, to do their best and feel proud of their contribution to the total effort.

    Much has been said about the work ethic—who has it, who doesn't. Commentators often bemoan the lack of a work ethic among so many employees. Actually, the work ethic is very strong, though today's younger workers have some different attitudes toward the importance of their work in their lives. They still want to do a good job, but they want the work to be more meaningful, more appreciated.

You don't have to start from "scratch". You already have a good starting point. Your challenge, your opportunity, is to energize what is *already present* in your organization, to implement the principles of *The Process of Excelling*, and to work with your people in positive ways to achieve your desired results.

Your people are receptive to the excelling message, but they want to hear it from you—in your own words, with your own fervor being clearly expressed. They're tired of the motivational lectures, tapes, signs, and notes. They want to see *your* passion . . . and they want to see you walk your talk.

The Enabling Steps

The first step is to develop your organization's mission statement. Remember, don't write it alone. This important work should be a *collaborative* effort. Not only will you benefit from input from others but people will become more committed to the process, the statement, and the fulfillment of the jointly-created mission.

All concerned must share the same purpose. If this conscious sharing doesn't occur, you and your people will be moving in different directions. Your productive energy will be dispersed and diminished. At least engage your key people in the exciting creativity process. Once the mission statement is clearly written and agreed upon, you're ready to begin conveying it to your all your stakeholders.

The communication of your mission is an internal marketing endeavor. Reach out to your people just as you reach out to your customers. *Sell* your mission statement and help each and every employee understand how his/her work contributes to the accomplishment of your mission. Note: divisions, departments, offices or other sub-units of the larger entity can also have their own missions . . . as long as their missions are congruent with the larger mission.

Mission accomplishment should be accomplished through fulfillment of established organizational goals and objectives. You can even use the mission statement itself as a stimulus to involve people in the process of developing goals and objectives. When they're part of the process, people will be much more supportive of the implementation and achievement of the desired results. As I emphasize in my speeches, "People support what they help to create."

The establishment of major organizational goals should be done by senior managers. You may want to invite input from middle managers and perhaps from junior managers, but the primary involvement in this longer-range and broader perspective phase should be at the higher level(s) of your team.

Once the overall goals are set, people from throughout the organization can become involved in setting the objectives to meet those goals. Subdivide each objective into concrete action steps to be taken by leaders and their direct reports. The action steps that follow will move you right into detailing the expectations of each member of your team.

As you move further into the creation of your total plan, continually involve more and more people at all levels of your organization. Get everyone involved! Create and feed the sense of *ownership*. Build commitment to the plan and its high quality implementation, and people will come forward to support what they helped to create. This exciting process helps build team strength as people gradually believe in—and subscribe—to their shared vision. The sharing of information and strategic design (focus) builds invaluable trust and understanding . . . and passion.

As a supportive manager, your next step should be to assure that each member of your team has the competence and confidence to achieve the expectations. It doesn't matter how clear the expectations are if the people don't know how to perform the required tasks. It's vital that everyone has confidence—in the plan and in his/her own ability to get the job done. If they don't believe it's right, or if they don't believe it's something they *can* do, their level of performance will be far below what you expect them to be.

Work with each of your subordinates on a one-on-one basis, encouraging them to stretch to perform at maximum levels. Teach them the skills and knowledge they need to achieve. Provide them with the support and other resources to get their job done. Then raise the bar. Encourage people to do even more. Engage consultants who can help you with this exciting growth process.

Give your employees feedback in a positive way to keep them striving to excel, personally and as a group. Personal attention, approval, caring, and other kinds of support and recognition will be more effective than monetary rewards.

You're appealing to your employees' desire to do a good job for the job's sake (internal reward), not for additional cash in their pockets (external reward).

Enable your people to see how their efforts contribute to the overall achievement of the team or organization. With each employee, focus on personal and professional future development. Help them grow to be of more value to themselves and to their employer through formal and informal learning experiences. Give them the support and inspiration they need to perform at their highest levels, then give them the freedom and opportunity to experience personal accomplishment.

Don't stop once you've started the process. Keep doing more of the same to maintain the momentum you've created. Modify plans and keep them up to date. Strengthen expectations of each member of the team as your people stretch to improve their performance.

Through the feedback and formal appraisal system, keep open your lines of communication concerning employee achievement and growth. Expect the best from your people, and you'll probably get it.

Overcoming Resistance

Don't be surprised if you encounter resistance as you begin your work to make needed changes in your organization. The resistance has been built up over many years, so don't take it personally. Your employees have been taught and socialized to behave in ways that are mediocre, compared to what can be accomplished by excelling. As you change, and encourage them to change, it's only natural that they will be suspicious.

Old behaviors are hard to change. The process will take time. You have to be patient, yet persistent. Many of the people you work with will be reluctant to change. They've gotten comfortable in their old ways, and things seem to be working all right. They may have difficulty accepting your suggestion that life will be better with the new ways of doing things.

To help people change, show them the relevance of the new style to their personal lives. Show them how the changes will affect them on an individual basis. Move slowly, yet persuasively, to help them understand, to visualize how life will be under the excelling approach.

Explain carefully and clearly what will be expected of them, and what they can expect from you. Help them appreciate how the changes will positively affect the entire organization, and that each person's participation is vital for the organization to excel as a whole. Let them know how they are needed, and how their personal involvement is significant.

As you read this, you may be wondering how you can convince some of your people to "go along with the program". As you proceed through the enabling steps, gradually getting more people involved, you will discover that the task becomes easier.

But, accept the reality that you may not be able to change everyone. Some people may even try to sabotage your efforts as some sort of plot or scheme against them. Amazingly, some people may feel threatened by your success, by your positive feelings toward achievement. Deal with each situation on an individual basis. In some cases, you'll need to work around the resistant people, hoping they will eventually join your efforts.

You may have to terminate employees who won't participate supportively in the excelling organization's activities. They won't be meeting the expectations of their employment, so you may have grounds for initiating disciplinary action with possible eventual termination.

Termination may seem drastic, particularly of employees who have been working for your organization for a long time. Obviously, you'd prefer not to take those steps, but you have to manage for the good of the organization. How will your increasingly productive team members feel if they have to work with someone who isn't doing his/her share?

Look carefully at those who resist; some of them may be low producers or non-producers who have managed to hide within the system. Even though they've been around for a long time, they really may be a costly detriment. Can you *afford* to carry them any longer?

Attitudes

Mental attitude is one of the major tenets of *The Process of Excelling*. While there are numerous techniques and practices to apply, a major factor is your attitude and the attitudes of other people in your organization. How you feel about your ability to excel, and whether you really want to, will spell the difference between your success and failure. Decide to be a winner, not a whiner.

You influence yourself and others with your attitudes. Your attitude is something that can't be faked or hidden. It will be reflected in what you say, how you think, and what you do. While attitudes are deeply imbedded within us, they show on the surface through our behavior.

To excel, your genuine attitude must be that you will always strive to do your best. You can't invest a half-hearted effort and expect top quality results. You have to sincerely believe in yourself and in your ability to achieve at increasingly higher levels. You have to consciously reach for what Charles Garfield and others describe as your "peak performance."

Realistically, you may not operate at your highest possible level of performance all the time. However, if your attitude and effort are focused in that direction, your achievement will be consistently higher.

Deliberately do those things that will help you, your people, and your organization to excel. Let that deliberateness begin deep inside you with the attitude that you will succeed; you will make a difference. When you encounter negative attitudes in yourself or in other people in your life, deliberately concentrate on changing those attitudes. Encourage a more productive and satisfying orientation of thinking and acting.

Recognize that what you are doing *is* meaningful. What you are doing makes a difference. As you begin applying the principles and techniques presented in this book, you will begin to see that difference. As you see it, share the feeling with your co-workers. Help them experience that same wonderful feeling that comes from positive change and achievement. Let everyone gain from the knowledge that what you're doing together really matters.

With your affirmative attitude will come dedication and commitment. Make a conscious commitment to excel, to do your best. Whenever appropriate, ask for the same commitment from others. As more and more people become deliberately and fully committed to excelling, you'll derive a wonderful satisfaction from the achievement of high performance.

Energizing your people and your organization is much like sending energy to a light bulb. As the light glows brighter and brighter, it provides both illumination and warmth. So it is with excelling attitudes and behavior. Now is the time to begin that energizing.

You can activate the switch that will send the energy of enthusiastic excelling flowing in your organization. Do it! Make it happen! Make a difference!

Thought-Provoking Questions

1. How will you begin installing *The Process of Excelling* in your organization?
2. What resistance do you anticipate in building an excelling organization? How will you overcome it?
3. What impact will your personal attitude have as you strive to build an excelling team? How can you manage that impact? How can you inspire excelling attitudes in each of your people?

Reader's Notes

19

Pride in Accomplishment

As your people and your organization practice excelling more and more, you will see some gratifying results. Take pride in your achievements! Share your pride with everyone who has made your excelling performance possible—your co-workers, suppliers, customers, and others. Thank them for their contributions, and offer ways to help them improve their performance in whatever they are doing.

Share your energy to light another's candle. As others around you become stronger, they will strengthen your position and your effectiveness. As the expression goes, "the rising tide lifts all boats." No one excels to his full potential alone. Consciously build your internal—and external—networks to enhance your current and future positioning. Reaching out to serve and support others as they serve and support you is collaborative servant leadership. The benefits are boundless. Excel together.

Excelling will become a new way of living, of working, in your organization. The powerful excelling thinking and attitudes generate enthusiastically positive and productive behaviors. It's contagious! People feed off each other's positive energy and accomplish wonderful things—for themselves, for their peers, for their superiors and subordinates, and for their employer, and for their "community" in the larger sense.

Getting excelling attitudes and behaviors initiated is only part of the picture. This refreshingly effective approach — lifestyle—is a phenomenon that has to be nurtured and reinforced. If not maintained, excelling behaviors can slip back to mediocrity. The atrophy can occur surprisingly fast. It's vital for success that your support of excelling performance be timely, sincere, and constant. It's a continuing process.

Striving for Mountaintop Performance

As a closing perspective, let's compare our performance to climbing a mountain. Far below us, at the foot of the mountain, is Poor Performance. While Poor Performances sometimes hard to see 'way down in the valley, we know it's always there in some form or another. Unfortunately, it's part of our lives.

People laboring in the Foothills of Poor Performance are well-satisfied with their substandard work. They have practically no motivation to expend effort on improving their performance. Some even avoid work whenever possible. They have no sense of ownership of their job or their results. They simply "attend" work. Each day is just like the one before: punch the clock, do what you're told, punch the clock, go home.

As we climb up our mountain—out of these depths of despair, the air becomes fresher and easier to breathe. We begin to feel a sense of accomplishment in our work. It may not be tremendously satisfying, but we're doing something. We are involved in some sort of productive activity. There's a reason to come to work. A sense of purpose underlies what we do. We feel a connection with others and with our achievement, modest though it may be.

A bit further up the mountain of performance, things seem to level out. It's not so difficult every day to show up and get something done. So workers do show up . . . and earn their "show up" pay. A significant number of people, often through no fault of their own, settle on the Plateau of Mediocrity. When they reach that point on their climb, they feel comfortable. They can breathe easily and enjoy a pleasant view. They know there's more mountain to climb, but don't have the motivation to invest more energy in continuing the climbing effort. There's no inspiration to achieve at a higher level. Complacency sets in.

If we look up, we can easily see that there's plenty of room at higher altitudes. If we become inspired to continue climbing, to move of that oh-so-comfortable plateau, there are greater rewards. The people we meet and work with at those loftier heights are internally driven and externally reinforced to consciously perform at higher levels. Those who are there feel especially good being there; it's both a conscious and a subconscious feeling.

At the top of the mountain is the peak, which we call "Excellence." The peak is hidden from our view by clouds. We know it's up there, but we aren't sure how far it is, what it looks like, or even how we'll know when we've arrived. We know intuitively that continuing the climb toward the peak is worth the effort. For excelling people, the climb is a natural process. It's just what we do.

Excelling, in this example, is our experience climbing up from the Plateau of Mediocrity towards the Peak of Excellence. Excelling is not a specific achievement; it is action. Excel is an active verb. We're "doing" something. We may not be exactly sure where we are on the mountain, but we do know that we're beyond the level of mediocrity. Even if we never reach the peak, the view is much better from up here. There's a definite feeling of exhilaration in knowing how far we've come, and knowing that we're still climbing!

We don't climb alone. Mountain climbing experts will tell you how foolish that is. There are others climbing with us (teamwork). We reach down to help others climb along with us (mentoring). We're really not worried about falling (attitude); we're using safety equipment as recommended (planning, goal setting with alternatives).

All of us who are climbing know where the others are. We know what we can expect from each other in terms of support and coordination (expectations). We know what we must do for ourselves, as well as for others (initiative, responsibility, accountability). We praise each other as we reach new heights (recognition), and encourage each other to keep climbing even when the going gets rough (inspiration, support). We're all working together (support groups) to excel at what we are doing.

We're not concerned about the mountaintop itself. Our attention and energy is focused on our climb. We have to give careful consideration to where we are now and where we're going next, or we'll lose control and perspective. In actual mountain-climbing, that loss of attention, loss of focus, could be fatal. In working with our organizations, a similar threat often hangs over us. It's vitally important to stay focused.

With the challenges of a rapidly changing world, it is imperative that we strive to excel—to do our best—in everything we do. Excelling at work alone won't be enough. We must make that commitment to excel professionally, organizationally, and personally, if we are to succeed. Yes, the same commitments that we make in our work environment apply to our home environment and our personal life. That consistency is essential for us to achieve congruence among the various facets of our lives.

Without conscious congruence, workers are doomed to a dangerous lack of balance in their lives. Those who fail to make that commitment, to balance their life activities and goals, probably won't succeed; they may not even survive. The need for life-balance has become all-consuming. We will be more driven by this desire, making major decisions like acceptance of job offers and decisions about where to live on the basis of achieving and maintaining balance. And that balance will be different for each of us.

You have the knowledge and the ability to excel—for yourself, for your team, and for your employer. All you have to do now is commit. Dedicate yourself to using all your personal and organizational resources to achieve the highest possible level of performance and achievement.

Now that you know the difference between excelling performance and get-by performance, your choice is clear. You can make your own decisions about what is best for your life.

The next move is yours.

Thought-Provoking Questions

1. Once you begin *The Process of Excelling* in your organization, how can you maintain the positive energy?
2. What can you do to assure that excelling behaviors are genuine, not just "lip service"?
3. With whom will you share the excitement of excelling? Job Applicants, suppliers, customers, stockholders, others? Why?
4. Are you satisfactorily in balance? If not, can you identify and gain what's missing?

Reader's Notes

About the Author

After 18 years of experience in management and sales in a variety of fields, Roger Herman entered the management consulting profession in 1980. His background includes work in manufacturing, distribution, retail, direct sales, and local government. He rose to serve at the top executive level in both private (Chief Executive Officer) and public (City Manager) sector organizations. His military service was in the capacity of a Counterintelligence Special Agent during the Viet Nam era.

As a Certified Management Consultant, Roger advises clients in a wide range of organizations throughout the United States and in a number of other countries. he gains insights and perspectives from an inside look at numerous companies, large and small. In addition to his personal experience, he learns from the experience of other consultants working for his firm, Herman Associates, Inc. (Greensboro, North Carolina), and his colleagues in his profession. Roger serves an an executive coach, primarily for business owners and senior executives.

In addition to his consulting, Roger interfaces with corporate leaders in his role as a professional speaker. The National Speakers Association recognizes him as one of fewer than 8 percent of its members to have earned the coveted Certified Speaking Professional designation. He delivers keynote speeches and seminars to corporate meetings and trade association conventions on a regular basis.

Roger holds a Bachelor of Arts degree in Sociology from Hiram College and a Master of Arts degree in Public Administration from the Ohio State University. He has completed a number of seminars, special courses, and other learning experiences and participates actively in his professional associations. Roger serves as a member of the Board of Directors of the Institute of Management Consultants.

If you'd like to engage Roger Herman as a consultant. speaker, or call Herman Associates at (910) 282–9370. fax number (910) 282–2003. His address is 3400 Willow Grove Court, Greensboro, North Carolina 27410–8600. You can reach him by e-mail at roger@herman.net or through his firm's web site, http://www. herman.net.

Index

C

D

E

involvement *(cont.)*
    employee, 66, 125, 131
    greater, 124
    increase level of, 122
    personal, 16, 123, 204
    positive, 121
    in trade associations, 159

K

knowledge, 20, 26, 49, 71, 202, 213
    sharing, 76, 174–176, 178
    visionary, 175

L

labor
    organized movement, 31
    unions, 31
leadership, 4, 10, 50, 112–114, 195, 199. *See also* teams,
    leadership
    dedicated, 186
    development, 122
    effectiveness, 103
    excelling, 97, 194
        style, 105
    lack of deliberate, 78
    level, 117
    management and, 77
    managership versus, 79–81
    need for, 182–183
    organization's, 49
    participative, 131
    phony, 199
    planned, 78

products *(cont.)*
    high quality, 185
    new, 50
    substandard, 30
productivity, 2
programs. *See also* Baldrige Award program; cash rewards
    education, 20, 167, 173
    employer-sponsored, 20
    motivational, 19
    non-cash incentive, 141
    performance incentive, 141
    retraining, 17
    suggestion, 16
    supervisory, 19
    technical, 19
    training, 16, 17, 19–20
        and development, 176
    worker safety, 122
promotion, ceremonial process, 18
protectionism, 29
    system of, 28
public school systems, 12
    performance, 12

Q

quality, 17–18, 122, 184
    excelling, 195
    level of, 193
    product, 185
    reputation, 196

R

re-engineering, 10
    corporate, 11